W9-COF-671

VOLUME 15

DISCOVERING ANTIQUES

THE STORY OF WORLD ANTIQUES

GREYSTONE PRESS/NEW YORK · TORONTO · LONDON

This superb full-color work is brought to you in its entirety from the original publisher, The British Publishing Corporation. Only the arrangement has been slightly altered. In fact, rather than disturb the text in any way, you will find the English monetary system used throughout the set. Here is a handy conversion table showing the value of a Pound (£) in terms of U.S. dollars.

DATES	U.S. Dollars equal to one Pound (£)
1939	$3.92 to 4.68
1940 to Sept. 1949	4.03
Sept. 1949 to Nov. 1967	2.80
Nov. 1967 to Aug. 1971	2.40
Aug. 1971 to June 1972	2.60
June 1972 to present	2.45 (floating rate)

20 shillings = one Pound (£)
21 shillings = one guinea

In February, 1971, the guinea was taken out of circulation.

TITLE PAGE PHOTO CREDIT: *Europa and the Bull,* style of Benvenuto Cellini, c. 1570. (National Gallery of Art, Washington.)

Published by the Greystone Press
225 Park Avenue South
New York, N.Y. 10003

Library of Congress Catalog Card Number: 72-90688

Cover Design: Harold Franklin

MANUFACTURED IN THE UNITED STATES OF AMERICA.

Contents

Giles Eyre

INDIA & THE RAJ

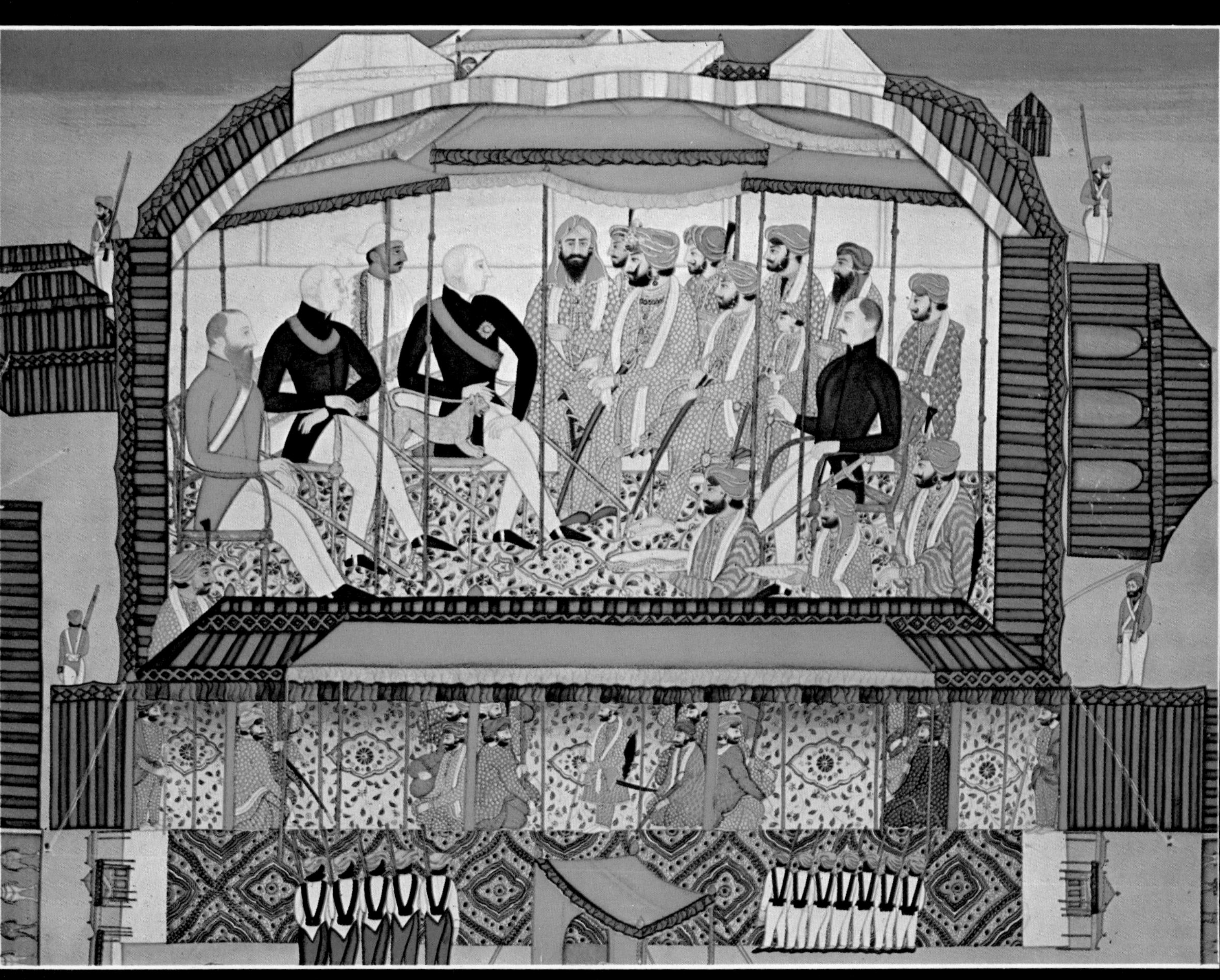

Fig. 1 ***The Lahore Durbar of 26 December, 1846***, *Sikh, Lahore, c.1846–47. Gouache. The Governor-General and his suite are seen here meeting the child Maharaja of the Punjab to ratify the Treaty of Lahore. The young Prince is surrounded by Sikh dignitaries. In the foreground are two attendants carrying trays of ceremonial presents. (British Museum, London.)*

Fig. 2 ***The Taj Mahal***, *near Agra, built by Shah Jahan (1592–1666) as a memorial to his much loved wife, 1630–53. This Emperor was overthrown by his son, Aurangzeb (1618–1707), who allowed him to see out his remaining years at Agra, gazing across at the magnificent edifice which had taken twenty-three years to complete. Both Shah Jahan and his wife were great patrons of the arts.*

Fig. 3 ***Colonel William Kirkpatrick*** *(1754–1812), British army officer and Persian scholar, by Thomas Hickey, c.1799. Oil. (National Gallery of Ireland, Dublin.)*

Fig. 4 ***A European in Indian dress smoking a hookah,*** *Lucknow School, c.1780–90. Gouache. (Hartnoll and Eyre Ltd., London.)*

By the nineteenth century the British had fully inherited the power to rule in India instituted by Akbar in the sixteenth century

The first phase of the Mughal conquest of India began in 1526, the year Henry VIII invited Holbein to England. Babur (1483–1530) was no ruthless conqueror, but a generous and civilised man, fond of music and the arts: they were, of course, Islamic arts, and particularly the arts of Persia.

The second phase of the conquest forced his son, Humayun (1508–56), to take refuge in Persia. He was an exile for sixteen years before he could return and recapture Delhi. Persian culture and a barbed political inheritance were left to his thirteen-year-old son, Akbar (1542–1605). It was in his time, the third and final phase of the Mughal conquest, that Elizabeth I granted a charter to the East India Company. While Akbar was building the Mughal edifice on the foundations provided by his grandfather, Babur, the penetration of India by Europeans had already begun.

The Mauryan Empire, the Guptas, Tughlak and the disintegration of the Delhi sultanate must have seemed well buried in the past when Akbar married a Rajput princess, who was to become the mother of the next Mughal emperor. Jahangir (1569–1627)

3

Museum Photo

4

A. C. Cooper

5

R. B. Fleming

6

A. F. Kersting

7

R. Todd-White

Fig. 5 ***The Burning Ghats at Benares*** *by Edward Lear (1812–88), 1873. Water-colour. Of the Ganges, Lear wrote, 'Utterly wonderful is the rainbow-like edging of the water with thousands of bathers reflected in the river . . . I find it one of the most abundantly* bruyant, *and startlingly radiant of places'. (India Office Library, London.)*

Fig. 6 ***The Diwan-e-Khas*** *in the Red Fort, Delhi, built by Shah Jahan. This was an abode of the Mughal emperors until the last was exiled to Rangoon in 1858.*

Fig. 7 ***Hira Singh*** *(c.1816–44), coloured lithograph from a sketch by Emily Eden, 1844. Hira Singh was the favourite of Ranjit Singh and was allowed to sit in the Maharajah's presence when this favour was denied even to his father, Raja Dhyan Singh. (Hartnoll and Eyre Ltd.)*

Fig. 8 ***Armed watchman*** *by George Chinnery, c.1810. Pen and ink. A sympathetic chronicler of Indian peasant life, Chinnery arrived in India in 1802. (India Office Library.)*

8

R. B. Fleming

Fig. 9 ***A Gentleman with his Hookah-Burdar, or Pipe-Bearer,*** *from* The Costume and Customs of Modern India *published by Captain Thomas Williamson from a collection of drawings by Charles D'Oyly, London, 1813. Engraving by J. H. Clark and C. Dubourg. Williamson states that 'Many are absolute slaves to their hookahs, which excepting while sleeping, or in the early parts of meals are ever at hand . . . (I) have ever found those, who were most bigotted to smoking, are the greatest dupes to their hookah burdars . . .'. (Victoria and Albert Museum, London.)*

Fig. 10 ***Marquis Wellesley and his Suite at the Nabob of Oude's breakfast table, viewing an elephant fight,*** *from* The Costume and Customs of Modern India, *see Figure 9. The Palace was at Lucknow, on the banks of the Gomati. (Victoria and Albert Museum.)*

9

K. Hoddle

10

K. Hoddle

was a man of taste, as much addicted to painting and music as to drugs and liquor. Possessed of fine aesthetic discrimination, and himself a painter, he was a patron of art and literature and, particularly, a lover of nature. He was also the lover and husband of Nur Jahan, whose great beauty was said to be as exquisite as her taste in Persian miniatures and poetry.

The Emperor valued Christian religious pictures above all others

A whole staff of craftsmen-artists worked in perfect collaboration at this Court, but it is significant that Jahangir valued Christian religious pictures above all others. We know from Sir Thomas Roe, the ambassador sent by James I to his Court at Agra, that, even when drunk, the Emperor would debate with pleasure the teachings of Jesus, Mohammed and Moses.

The reign of Shah Jahan (1592–1666), the victorious son of Jahangir who built the great palace fort at Delhi, is to be considered the golden period of Mughal rule, but there were shadows in the picture which were ignored. As in France under *le Roi Soleil*, the military system was growing weaker and the revenue administration more lax. He was overthrown by his son, Aurangzeb (1618–1707), who allowed him to spend his remaining years at Agra, gazing across at his wife's tomb, the Taj Mahal.

Aurangzeb, unlike his ancestors, was a bigot. He imposed a poll-tax on unbelievers and ignored the feelings of important Hindu sections of his people. Political progress depended on a policy of religious toleration which would seek to create harmony in a country of essentially discordant elements. His weak successors only hastened the process of decay. When Aurangzeb died, the British were already established in Madras, Bombay and Calcutta. The latter was in the heart of the richest province of the Mughal Empire, but its existence was precarious and much dependent upon presents to the Viceroy of Bengal: 'Clocks and watches that strike and have chimes you must by all means send . . .', and the servants of the Company sent them. But they had more than experience of oriental diplomacy; they had confidence gained both as administrators and as soldiers.

English portrait-painters began to be attracted to India

Sixty years later, when Clive had defeated another Viceroy of Bengal, he accepted, on behalf of the Company, the administration of the whole province in the Emperor's name. Thus the British took their place in the line of succession of those representatives who had first been appointed by Akbar.

It is in the second half of the eighteenth century that English portrait-painters began to be attracted to India. Tilly Kettle, John Zoffany and the Scotsman George Willison were all said to have made their fortune in Bengal or Madras. They painted the native rulers, the successful merchants and the most famous of the East India Company servants. When Ozias Humphry arrived in Calcutta in 1785, it was suggested to him that portrait-painting had been somewhat overdone and that he would be wise to confine himself to miniatures. He visited the Courts of Murshidabad, Benares and Lucknow, but the gold was already beaten a little thinner and he was not always paid for his work.

The period of corruption was nearly over

The period of corruption, when nawabs were kept as a mere pageant, was nearly over, and a time was coming when the sub-continent would be administered by a civil service whose integrity and concern for the welfare of the Indians was unprecedented. The year before Ozias Humphry had landed, William Hodges was on his way home with a collection of Indian landscapes; the year after, Thomas Daniell came out with his nephew, William. They were the first to record the magnificence of the Himalayas and the rocky beauty of the southern landscape as far as Cape Cormorin. In 1802, George Chinnery landed in Madras. He was in India for almost a quarter of a century and learned to love the country, not merely for its 'picturesque' or 'sublime' qualities, but because he found its people sympathetic; he knew their villages and never tired of sketching the broken pots, mud huts and bullock-carts of the *mofussil* (rural localities).

More importantly, he was an able and enthusiastic teacher. One of his pupils was Charles D'Oyly, who became the Company's opium agent at Patna in 1821. His duties were not unduly onerous and, by 1824, he had started an art society – the first that we know of in India – and ordered a lithographic press from England.

D'Oyly found a Murshidabad artist who had migrated to Patna and trained him to work the lithographic press and transfer the drawings of the art society on to stone. His name was Jairam Das, and he would probably have been surprised to know that he was instrumental in the bringing together of Indian and British culture.

By the middle of the nineteenth century, peace had been brought to the country and, instead of anarchy, the fields had been mapped out, the revenue established and a beginning had been made to the task of building roads and railways and of harnessing the rivers to irrigation. The British were no longer traders who blended with Indian society, adopted Indian habits and drew in her medieval culture from a hookah. Political power freed them from the need to associate, especially in the cities; and the increasing numbers of women encouraged them to lead a life insulated from contact with the Indian. In any case, for many, India was merely a stage in a long journey that would take them back to England.

Surrounded by the remains of 'a more perfect art'

Yet, there were important exceptions: men who studied Sanskrit, investigated ancient Hindu law and literature, studied natural history and observed sympathetically the manners and customs of the people. It would be unfair to suggest that these exceptions were confined to men. Emily Eden, the sister of Lord Auckland, Governor-General from 1836 to 1842, was particularly fascinated. 'I have had two Delhi miniature painters here, translating two of my sketches into ivory, and I never saw anything so perfect . . . Azim, the best painter, is almost a genius . . .', she reported in her diary. She made hundreds of sketches and paintings when she was on tour and bought as many native works as she could afford.

Yet, in the main, the Indian miniature technique received cautious approval. 'The specimens of Hindu art I have seen', wrote Maria Graham, 'are minute imitations of nature, on a scale in general more diminutive than our common miniatures; but there is a delicacy of handling about them that seems like the remains of a more perfect art'.

The remains of a more perfect art they had all around them. John Beames in his *Memoirs of a Bengal Civilian*, written between 1858 and 1893, did not mention one of them. In 1874 he would have been too busy dealing with a famine in Bihar to have noticed that the Viceroy, Lord Northbrook, had packed Edward Lear off to Benares. 'Got a boat', wrote Lear, 'a large one, for no one can have the least idea of this Indian city's splendour without this arrangement. Utterly wonderful is the rainbow-like edging of the water with thousands of bathers reflected in the river. Then the colour of the temples, the strangeness of the huge umbrellas and the inexpressibly multitudinous detail of the architecture . . . well I remember the views of Benares by Daniell; pallid, grey, sad and solemn . . . Instead, I find it one of the most abundantly *bruyant*, and startlingly radiant of places . . . Constantinople or Naples are simply dull and quiet by comparison'.

'The moon . . . shone over the Ganges and touched the shrinking channels into threads of silver'

Perhaps this was the trouble; the British always wanted to compare India with somewhere else. The Himalayas were like Switzerland; Kashmir like the Lake District; Ootacamund like Surrey. The very nice Lady Mellanby in E. M. Forster's *A Passage to India*, who offered Mrs. Moore – an unknown and obscure old inhabitant – accommodation in her own reserved cabin home, was perhaps typical; but then, so too perhaps was Mrs. Moore. 'Mrs. Moore had always inclined to resignation. As soon as she landed in India, it seemed to her good . . . As she left Chandrapore the moon, full again, shone over the Ganges and touched the shrinking channels into threads of silver . . . The swift and comfortable mail-train slid with her through the night . . . She watched the indestructible life of man and his changing faces, and the houses he had built for himself and God, and they appeared to her not in terms of her own trouble but as things to see. There was, for instance, a place called Asigarh which she passed at sunset and identified on a map – an enormous fortress among wooded hills . . . "I have not seen the right places", she thought, as she was embayed in the platforms of the Victoria Terminus the end of the rails that had carried her over a continent and could never carry her back . . . As she drove through the huge city which the West had built and abandoned with a gesture of despair, she longed to stop, although it was only Bombay . . . Then the steamer rounded Colaba, the continent swung about, the cliff of the Ghats melted into the haze of a tropic sea. Lady Mellanby turned up and advised her not to stand in the heat: "We are safely out of the frying-pan", said Lady Mellanby, "it will never do to fall into the fire"'.

Furniture in India

Veronica Murphy

Raymond Fortt

Using fine local materials such as teak, sandalwood and ivory, Indian craftsmen of the eighteenth century made distinctive variations on European patterns

A. C. Cooper

Before the coming of Europeans to India, furniture was scarcely known there. Chairs, for example, were not used; rulers sat on elaborately carved thrones and everyone else on the floor, although the rich indulged themselves with carpets and cushions. During the sixteenth and early seventeenth centuries, with the founding of the various East India Companies which were intended to exploit the riches of the East, Europeans – first the Portuguese, followed by the English and the Dutch – began to arrive and to establish trading settlements along the west and east coasts. Some of these settlements rapidly expanded into prosperous towns.

Among the basic requirements of the colonists was furniture, a commodity which could not easily be transported from Europe on overcrowded ships, on which cargo space was needed for trade goods and essential supplies. It was soon discovered that Indian craftsmen had a remarkable ability to copy meticulously even totally unfamiliar articles, as long as some kind of pattern was provided.

This fact was attested by numerous observers over a period of centuries. One eyewitness, the naval surgeon Edward Ives, wrote that the 'mechanics' only ask for '*muster*, that is, for a pattern, and they will be sure to keep exactly to it, be the fashion thereof never so extravagant . . . It is astonishing how exactly they will copy anything you give them, although they scarce know the use of ten tools, and although the few they have are always in bad condition . . . they are most admirable copyists'. He was referring to Madras in 1754, but the same would have been true of

Fig. 1 ***Cabinet on stand**, east Indian (Vizagapatam), late eighteenth century. Rosewood and ivory. (Victoria and Albert Museum, London.)*

Fig. 2 ***Revolving chair**, east Indian (Vizagapatam), probably c.1770. Wood. (Victoria and Albert Museum.)*

Indian Furniture

Fig. 3 **Writing-box on table,** *east Indian (Vizagapatam), mid-eighteenth century. Rosewood, inlaid with incised ivory.*
These scaled-down versions of the European bureau, usually fitted with a carrying-handle on each side, were produced in fairly large numbers. The table on which it stands could date from the seventeenth century, but its inlaid decoration is closely related to that on the bureau. Indian furniture often has a slightly antiquated appearance, due to the copying of out-of-date designs. (Victoria and Albert Museum.)

3

Museum Photo

4

A. C. Cooper

Fig. 4 **Armchair,** *probably south Indian (Mysore), second half of the eighteenth century. Carved from solid ivory, with painted and gilt decoration.*
This comes from a large suite of matching furniture reputed to have belonged to Tipu Sahib, Sultan of Mysore, and to have been among the trophies of Seringapatam in 1799. (Victoria and Albert Museum.)

Fig. 5 ***Toilet-glass and stand of stepped drawers,*** *east Indian (Vizagapatam), late eighteenth century. Sandalwood, veneered with incised ivory.*
This piece is thought to have been acquired by Lt.-Col. George Roberts in about 1792. (Victoria and Albert Museum. Lent by Mrs. D. E. Bromley.)

almost any town and period.

Thus, from the beginning of European colonisation, many craftsmen perhaps previously engaged in making wooden house-fittings or as hereditary wood- and ivory-carvers for the local temple, found employment in making furniture for the newcomers. Since the Portuguese were the first Europeans to settle in India, many sixteenth- and seventeenth-century pieces of Indo-European furniture are associated with Goa, the Portuguese colony on the south-west coast. Other seventeenth- and early eighteenth-century articles reflect the period of Dutch ascendancy in South India and Ceylon. Whatever the initial source of inspiration, it was only in outline that this furniture copied its European prototypes. Many of the decorative details, whether in wood, ivory or mother of pearl, carved or inlaid, were unmistakably Indian, and it is this fusion of Eastern and Western elements which constitutes the attraction of such furniture.

Over the years, several schools of furniture-making developed in different parts of the country, most of them displaying strong regional characteristics. The three vital factors governing the emergence of these schools were the availability of raw materials (e.g., wood and ivory), the presence of craftsmen and the arrival of European patrons. Occasionally timber was brought a considerable distance by sea or river. The schools making extensive use of ivory tended to be within easy reach of jungle tracts where elephants could be found. Craftsmen were sometimes persuaded to migrate from declining areas to those where employment might be expected, such as the centres of European influence, which, during the eighteenth century, passed largely into the hands of the British. Hence, much surviving furniture of the period is based on English designs.

By this time, Indian craftsmen had been making European-style furniture for about two hundred years, which may explain why so much of their eighteenth-century work is highly satisfactory, from both aesthetic and technical viewpoints.

A characteristic of all the schools, of whatever period, is the extensive use made of wooden pegs (or ivory in the case of ivory furniture) in joints, or to attach veneers. Often, some of these pegs have been replaced by screws at a later date. The

6

7

Fig. 6 ***Table,*** *probably south Indian (Mysore), late eighteenth century. Wood, veneered with ivory; relief decoration in carved and gilt ivory.* *(Victoria and Albert Museum.)*

Fig. 7 ***Combined games- and work-table,*** *west Indian (Bombay or Surat), early nineteenth century. Wood, veneered with ivory inlaid with a geometrical mosaic of tin, stained ivory, wood and horn. Decorated with complex 'Bombay inlaid work', this box is fitted with needlework implements as well as games pieces. 'Bombay boxes' were among the effects of Queen Charlotte auctioned by Christie's after her death in 1819. (Messrs. Phillips of Hitchin (Antiques) Ltd., Hertfordshire.)*

pegs were necessary because the casein adhesive used in India instead of glue tended to dry out.

Another hallmark of Indian furniture, particularly ivory, is the utilisation of odd pieces, pegged together to build up a section. It is understandable in the case of ivory, which is inclined to become brittle and to split when being worked, but off-cuts of wood were also treated in this way.

A third characteristic is that chairs and settees were invariably cane-seated for coolness. The canework was often replaced with upholstery when such chairs found their way to Europe, but examination of the seat-frames will reveal the holes where the canes were attached.

Furniture of the Vizagapatam school, on the east coast, is probably the most familiar of the eighteenth-century Indian products (see Figs. 1, 2, 3 and 5). Often wrongly described in catalogues as 'Goanese' or 'Indo-Portuguese', it falls into two main divisions. First is the furniture of Asian hardwood (rosewood, ebony or teak were the most used), inlaid with ivory, which was in its turn inlaid with black lac applied in a molten state to incised designs scratched on the surface. The ivory motifs were prepared by carving a section of tusk in the required shape all down its length, then slicing it into a number of thin, identical, transverse sections. These shapes were placed on the wood, roughly sketched round, and the corresponding piece of wood removed, to be replaced by ivory. Any gaps were filled with lac, coloured to match the surrounding wood. The incising and lac-filling of the ivory sections were sometimes carried out before, sometimes after, inlaying.

The decoration usually consists of a border design of stylised flowers, deriving from Indo-Persian textiles, but sometimes incorporating European marquetry patterns. Less commonly occurs the 'Flowering Tree', with its rockery, birds and animals, so well known in the painted cottons of the Coromandel Coast, below Vizagapatam.

The other speciality of Vizagapatam consisted of veneering sheets of ivory on a wooden core, the veneered surface then being incised and lac-filled, as with inlaid pieces. When chairs were decorated in this way, the framework was often of teak, chosen for its stability. One such chair is the so-called 'Burgomaster' type (Fig. 2). Its incised ornament includes stiff floral sprigs, which appear to derive from a European embroidery pattern-book of the seventeenth century, and, on the knees, acanthus leaves which cleverly simulate carving. Despite the old-fashioned appearance of the revolving upper half (unchanged from seventeenth-century models), its cabriole legs place it firmly in the eighteenth century, perhaps as late as 1770, since its incised ornament is almost identical to that on a set commissioned by Governor Wynch of Madras at that time.

Towards the turn of the century, a staple product of the Vizagapatam workshops was 'beautiful sandalwood and ivory boxes, for which the place is famous'. So they were described by

8

A. C. Cooper

Fig. 8 ***Portrait** showing a European artist seated on a veneered ivory chair, painting a group portrait of Shuja-al-daula, Nawab of Oudh, and his family at Lucknow, c.1772. Painted by an unknown Indian artist, this water-colour is thought to be a copy of an oil, now lost, by the English painter Tilly Kettle, in which he depicted himself at work. The copy may have been commissioned by Richard Strachey, British Resident at Lucknow between 1815 and 1817.*
(Victoria and Albert Museum.)

Mrs. Eliza Fay on her arrival there on 30 January, 1796. Though larger items were probably always specially commissioned, it seems that a plentiful supply of small boxes, tea-chests, portable writing-desks, etc., was available ready made. Ships sailing for England from Calcutta would put into the port so that homeward-bound Britons could buy souvenirs. Figure 5 shows a sandalwood and ivory toilet-glass of Mrs. Fay's period. Sandalwood was highly valued for the permanence of its scent.

Another school appears to have existed in the southern state of Mysore. This is puzzling, since the *de facto* rulers of Mysore during the second half of the eighteenth century were Haidar Ali and his son Tipu – the celebrated 'Tiger of Mysore' – who were implacable enemies of the British. Yet a number of reasonably authenticated pieces of basically English design, in ivory, both carved and veneered (Figs. 4 and 6) were probably made in Mysore at that time. The ivory and the craftsmen were available, but Haidar and Tipu seem rather improbable patrons of such furniture. On the other hand, we do know from contemporary accounts that Western-style fittings were among the furnishings of the palace at Seringapatam.

Ivory was extensively worked in Bengal; European-style furniture was made there at Kasimbazaar and Berhampur, suburbs of Murshidabad. Warren Hastings, Governor-General of Bengal in 1772, was presented with a costly set of chairs, settees, tables and footstools by the widow of the local nawab. He also owned, and greatly prized, an ivory bed. Unfortunately, very little Bengal furniture is known for certain to have survived. English people sometimes referred scathingly to the 'brittle and flimsy' qualities of local ivory products, and the only piece with an impeccable pedigree is a small Adamesque work-table, with slender screw-on legs, which, although pleasing to the eye, can be said to merit such criticism. The Bengal craftsmen both carved and veneered ivory. They also made ebony furniture, but no eighteenth-century specimens are recorded.

Even more elusive is the Patna furniture, a commonplace of life in Bengal, to judge from the frequent references to it. Two entries in the *Calcutta Gazette*, on Thursday, 5 August and Thursday, 4 November, 1784, both announce items to be sold at auction: 'A handsome set of Patna furniture for a bedroom, painted green and silver', and 'Patna common chairs, couches and teapoys'. None of this has been identified; it may have been turned and decorated with coloured lac.

Furniture was also made at Bombay and Surat, which were among the earliest English settlements in India. Colonel James of the Madras Army, visiting Surat in 1804, wrote: 'Nearly fifty thousand are Parsees, who are the principal artisans: carpenters, joiners . . . turners, etc.; it was quite a treat to me, to see them at work with European tools, and in an European manner, and really they were remarkably moderate in their charges . . .'.

Colonel James may have bought some of the popular 'Bombay inlaid work' shown in Figure 7. This mosaic inlay, manufactured in pre-shaped bundles and then cut into thin transverse slips, rather like Tunbridge ware, has been made for centuries in Mediterranean and Arab countries. It came to India from Persia, and throughout the nineteenth century was made at Bombay and Surat to decorate furniture and a great variety of small wares for European use. It is often found applied to carved sandalwood work-boxes. The early example of the technique seen in the games- and work-table shown here conforms more closely to eighteenth-century tradition than to most products of nineteenth-century Indo-European taste. This was typified by 'Bombay blackwood' furniture, massive, heavily carved and French polished.

MUSEUMS AND COLLECTIONS

Although most Indian furniture is still in private ownership, examples may be seen at the following:

GREAT BRITAIN

Derby: Kedleston Hall
London: Sir John Soane's Museum
Victoria and Albert Museum
Welshpool: Powis Castle

NETHERLANDS

Amsterdam: Rijksmuseum

FURTHER READING

'Art and the East India Trade: Some Little-Known Ivory Furniture' by Veronica Murphy, **Connoisseur,** December, 1970.
'The Indian Period of European Furniture' by R. Edwards and K. de B. Codrington, **Apollo,** February/April and June/July, 1935.

1

A. C. Cooper

Skills of the Indian Craftsman

Robert Skelton

Fig. 1 **Lime-box,** *Ceylon, early nineteenth century. Brass, cast in two halves with a hinge at the feet and a ring for suspension from the waist. Resembling the supporting lions of pillars in south Indian temples, this box is a container for lime, used in the preparation of betel for chewing. (Victoria and Albert Museum, London.)*

The variety of materials, including glass, ivory, wood and stones, combined with the superb quality of the workmanship, place the decorative arts of India among the finest in the world

In the early years of the twentieth century, interest in the decorative arts of India was eclipsed by the sudden recognition by western critics that Indian sculpture and painting comprised more than grotesque fantasy clothed in occasional virtuosity; they pronounced them to be a valid expression of the human spirit, with masterpieces worthy to stand beside those of any other culture. Almost at once the examples of Indian craftsmanship popularised by the great exhibitions of the nineteenth century, eulogised in books and journals and cherished in Victorian drawing-rooms, became disregarded as unfashionable knick-knacks.

If we look at the literature on Indian art we can see how great a reversal of opinion took place. Nineteenth-century British writers scarcely admitted the existence of the fine arts in India, but they lavished unstinted praise on the industrial arts and accumulated a great deal of valuable information about them. The classic work of this genre was Sir George Birdwood's *The Industrial Arts of India*, published in 1880. With one or two others, it is still a standard work, for there has been no serious attempt to break fresh ground on a comprehensive scale since Sir George Watt catalogued the handicrafts shown in Delhi in 1903. Recent general studies by Indian writers are almost entirely based on these nineteenth-century surveys, and handicrafts are now treated with as little attention as the fine arts received in Victorian times. Many excellent examples of nineteenth-century Indian craftsmanship have survived, however, and a revival of interest in these decorative arts is due and can reasonably be expected.

In view of this, it is unfortunate that the very period when Indian handicrafts enjoyed their greatest acclaim and received extensive documentation was, in fact, the moment of their decline. As in most countries, the decorative arts of India have depended for their sustenance on the co-existence of deep-rooted and vigorous popular traditions, together with informed aristocratic patronage. In the eighteenth and nineteenth centuries these supporting forces sustained a number of shocks from which they never fully recovered.

The decline of the Mughal Empire seriously reduced the stimulus that was formerly provided by a wealthy and ostentatious Court, whose nobility emulated the aesthetic values of a cultivated dynasty. In 1739 Delhi was sacked by the invader Nadir Shah, who carried away many of its

Fig. 2 **Coffee-pot,** *Kashmir, late eighteenth century. Copper with chased decoration. (Victoria and Albert Museum.)*

Fig. 3 **Lamp (Dipa Lakshmi)** *in the form of the Goddess of Fortune, whose torso acts as a reservoir from which oil drips as the tray empties, south Indian, early nineteenth century. Brass. (Victoria and Albert Museum.)*

Fig. 4 **Bottle,** *from the collection of Lord Clive, eighteenth century. Carved jade set with gold and gems. (By permission of Mrs. D. Schreiber.)*

2

A. C. Cooper

3

A. C. Cooper

treasures and craftsmen to Persia. With the central authority thus weakened, politically dynamic but culturally unsophisticated marauders unleashed their armies in provinces which had formerly been stable and prosperous. Craftsmen were still patronised at Courts such as Lucknow, but standards in taste declined severely. In the meantime, British power in India increased as a result of both rivalry with France in Europe and a need for stable conditions under which to pursue an Eastern trade which was becoming ever more lucrative. No sooner did the Indian craftsman bless his new rulers for removing the sources of anarchy, than he found them changing the whole structure of patronage, flooding the market with their manufactured goods and introducing their own alien notions of design. Thus, by the time Birdwood and Watt were compiling their studies of Indian handicrafts, the fabric of Indian urban life from which the crafts sprang was undergoing deep social changes, even though the rural population appeared to remain in its age-old traditional mould.

In the cities, craftsmen adapted to the new circumstances but certain of the luxury crafts dependent on court patronage died out almost completely. The rajahs and nawabs were among the first to emulate European taste, and they devoted themselves to the acquisition of French furniture, crystal chandeliers and European oil-paintings, rather than to supporting the work of indigenous craftsmen. As if these revised attitudes on the part of Indian patrons were not enough to confuse the artisans, there were also newly founded art schools run by Englishmen to replace the traditional system of craft training based on hereditary occupational castes.

In view of all these pressures, it is remarkable that indigenous traditions retained their character and vitality for as long as they did. Certain of the crafts in this period clearly reflect the effects of compromise with the new influences, but in some cases there is no evidence of adulteration. This is particularly evident in south Indian metalwork. The figure of a lamp-bearer in Figure 3 is a direct descendant of the great south Indian temple images cast in bronze by the *cire perdue* (lost wax) process.

The ornamental style of the great south Indian temples was simulated in objects for domestic use

This technique, in which the figure is modelled in wax and then covered with a clay mould from which the wax is melted out before pouring in the molten metal, was already practised in India four thousand years ago. It reached perfection in the south by the tenth century A.D. under the Chola dynasty in a series of images which combined subtle naturalism with intense spiritual insight. Although the lamp-bearer lacks these qualities and shows the stylisation of form characteristic of the later medieval period, it still retains a plastic and rhythmic energy that even earlier bronzes sometimes lack.

Lamps of this kind were, of course, used in a religious context, and their design may be expected to have resisted change, but the ornamental tradition preserved in the decoration of the great south Indian temples was also copied in objects for domestic use. An example is provided by the brass lion in Figure 1, which resembles the pillar-bases of south Indian temples from the seventh century A.D. This is a container for lime, which is used in the preparation of betel for chewing. It was made in Ceylon, the artistic traditions of which are closely derived from those of south India.

The same decorative influences are present in the south, even when the techniques appear to be of more recent and external origin. The famous 'swami work' of Tanjore (Fig. 5) is decorated with figures of the gods represented in arched niches as they appear in stone on the walls of temples. The inlay technique of silver on copper is probably intrusive in the area, but the decoration of the chased and repoussé silver foil hammered into the engraved outlines of the design is indigenous. Although it has been modified by local craft practice in this instance, the inlay techniques so commonly found in Indian metalwork are probably of Near Eastern origin and adopted as a result of the Muslim invasions.

This is certainly true of another celebrated ware, which takes its name, 'Bidri', from Bidar, the capital of a Muslim kingdom in the Deccan, where this particular form of metal inlay was first produced. These wares are cast in an alloy containing various combinations of zinc, lead, tin and copper. Silver is inlaid into the chased surface, and the alloy is then blackened by applying a mixture of salts, such as sal-ammoniac and saltpetre.

Although Bidri ware came to be produced at a number of centres, the decoration always betrays its Muslim origin. The coffee-pot illustrated in Figure 2 is even more pronounced in its Near Eastern inspiration, in form and decoration, as well as technique. This was made in Kashmir, where chased-copper vessels were made in a style popular in Persia from the Safawid period onwards. The earlier Kashmir examples could easily be confused with Persian work but, by the middle of the nineteenth century, both the execution and the decoration had acquired strong local characteristics. As in Persia, this type of copper-work was often tinned, or even gilt, in rather a garish manner.

Because of their proximity to Iran, the craftsmen of Kashmir owed a greater debt to Persian artistic traditions than did those of any other part of India. This was particularly true in the eighteenth and nineteenth centuries, when Near Eastern influences introduced elsewhere under the Sultans and Mughal emperors were being assimilated into the native tradition. Despite this, a strong regional decorative tradition grew up in Kashmir during the nineteenth century in which motifs of Persian or Mughal origin were treated in a distinctive manner. Arabesques became dominated by wildly flowing, rhythmic, S-shaped curves, which led to extravagant variations of the so-called 'cone' motif, featured particularly in nineteenth-century Kashmir shawls and their Paisley copies. This 'Paisley pattern' is also characteristic of Kashmir painted and lacquered woodwork or papier mâché – crafts which were introduced from Persia and became mainly localised in Kashmir and Sind (Fig. 9).

The principal stimulus which led to the introduction of crafts from Iran was the growth of the Mughal Empire in the sixteenth century.

Fig. 5 ***Water-vessel**, Tanjore, nineteenth century. Copper encrusted with silver repoussé decoration (swami work).* (Victoria and Albert Museum.)

Fig. 6 ***Base for a hookah**, made in a Mughal court workshop, beginning of the eighteenth century. Gilt glass.* (Victoria and Albert Museum.)

Fig. 7 ***A European officer, an Indian nobleman and a rocket-bearer**, models made for the Rajah of Peddapur, northern Madras State, late eighteenth century. Brass.* (Victoria and Albert Museum.)

Fig. 8 ***Turban-ornament**, Jaipur, early nineteenth century. Gold decorated with champlevé enamel.* (Victoria and Albert Museum.)

The Mughals came originally from the Turanian Plain (an area in Russia immediately north of Persia), but they owed their cultural background to Persia and gave personal encouragement to the development of crafts which stemmed from this foreign heritage. In many cases, the basic craft techniques were already familiar to Hindu craftsmen but, as Emperor Akbar's prime minister wrote of textiles in the late sixteenth century: 'Skilful masters and workmen have settled in this country, to teach people an improved system of manufacture'.

An instance of this is the development of glass manufacture, which was known in India from early times but had never been developed to a very high level of craftsmanship. Even under the Mughals, a great deal of the finer quality glass used in India was imported from Europe; locally made glass of Mughal design was also used, and it shows clear technical and decorative affinities with Persian glass of the Safawid period (Fig. 6). Jade-carving was similarly introduced to India from Persia or Turkestan at the beginning of the seventeenth century, although the technical methods employed were little different from those with which Indian craftsmen had carved rock crystal for some two millenia. Obviously some advances in technique were necessary to satisfy the Imperial taste for fine quality, but it is mainly the introduction of the new material (nephrite) and the copying of new forms and decorative motifs which constitutes the outside influence. In this instance, the Mughal craftsmen soon excelled their mentors and left the imported designs behind in favour of more imaginative and often organic forms. A characteristic of later Mughal jades is the inlay of gold and precious stones, already pioneered in the Near East, which gave the material a sumptuous effect suited to its use for objects of luxury. This craft was still flourishing when Lord Clive was laying the foundations of British power (Fig. 4), but it did not survive the withdrawal of patronage by the Mughal nobility in the nineteenth century.

The related craft of jewellery manufacture survived these social changes due to the long-standing Indian practice of hoarding wealth in the form of gold and precious stones. The goldsmith has, in fact, been an important member of Indian community life from the earliest times, and detailed regulations governing the craft have survived from a state manual of the Mauryan period

4

Author's Photo

5

A. C. Cooper

6

A. C. Cooper

7

A. C. Cooper

8

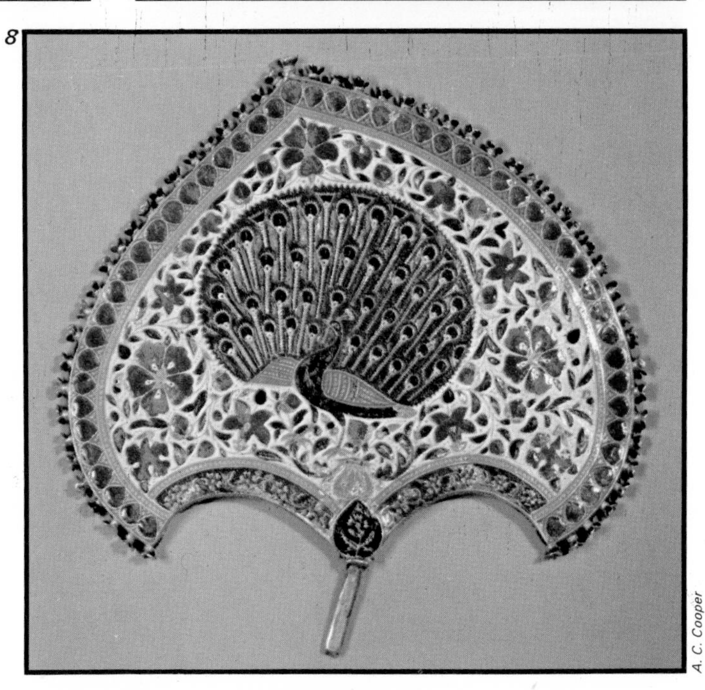

A. C. Cooper

Fig. 9 ***Box**, Kashmir, mid-nineteenth century. Painted and lacquered wood. A strong regional tradition grew up in Kashmir during the nineteenth century in which motifs of Persian or Mughal origin were treated in a distinctive manner. Extravagant variations of the so-called 'cone' motif were often featured in Kashmir shawls of the period and in their Paisley copies. This 'Paisley pattern' is also characteristic of Kashmir painted and lacquered woodwork or papier mâché. (Victoria and Albert Museum.)*

(fourth to third centuries B.C.). It is curious, however, that, despite the investment element in jewellery manufacture, the stones used were employed for their rich effect rather than for their purity, and it is not uncommon to find synthetic or semi-precious stones used alongside others of much greater value. Much of the gold jewellery is of thin metal on a lac foundation, and the stones are invariably cut and polished *en cabochon* rather than faceted.

In northern India, from the sixteenth century onwards, personal ornaments and certain objects of court use were often decorated with champlevé enamel, which was perhaps introduced to the Court of Akbar by Persian craftsmen. Similarities with the *basse taille* enamel of contemporary European court workshops suggest, however, that European craftsmen at the Mughal Court may have contributed to the development of this craft in India.

Its chief centre today is Jaipur, where examples of the best current work are indistinguishable from nineteenth-century pieces. It has been claimed that enamellers moved to Jaipur from the Mughal Court in the sixteenth century, but this is clearly untrue, and the earliest Jaipur pieces are not likely to have been made before the eighteenth or early nineteenth century (Fig. 8).

Jaipur also appears to have been the home of another craft which is the subject of an unfounded tradition by recent writers. This is the manufacture of a specific type of painted ivory chess-set which tends nowadays to be attributed to Madras (Fig. 10). Ivory-carving is one of the oldest Indian crafts, with a wide distribution all over the sub-continent. Early examples possess all the organic vitality of temple sculpture, but many nineteenth-century examples, particularly from Berhampore, Bengal, show this traditional skill being wasted on lifeless realism. The Jaipur pieces, by contrast, possess a gay charm related to the qualities of Rajput folk art. As in the case of Bengal sets made for the British, the pieces often represent East India Company sepoys opposed by native troops.

The humour displayed in the characterisation of such small military figures is even more manifest in a remarkable series of brass toys said to have been made for the Rajah of Peddapur in the late eighteenth century (Fig. 7). Unlike most south Indian brass-work, these figures show evidence of realistic observation which is undoubtedly due to some form of European contact. In date, they belong to the period when the British were only on the threshold of power in India, but already in terms of India's artistic tradition these delightful figures are a sinister portent of the final collapse.

9

A. C. Cooper

10

A. C. Cooper

Fig. 10 ***Chess-set**, Jaipur, early nineteenth century. Painted ivory carved to represent East India Company and native sepoy armies. Unlike the lifeless ivory figures of nineteenth-century Bengal, those from Jaipur always possess a gay charm related to the qualities of Rajput folk art. (Victoria and Albert Museum.)*

FURTHER READING

The Handicrafts and Industrial Arts of India by R. J. Mehta, Bombay, 1960.
Indian Art at Delhi, 1903 by G. Watt, Calcutta, 1903.
The Industrial Arts of India by G. C. M. Birdwood, London, 1884.
The Journal of Indian Art (and Industry), London, 1884–1916.

MUSEUMS AND COLLECTIONS

Indian decorative arts may be seen at the following:

FRANCE
Paris: Musée Guimet

GREAT BRITAIN
Edinburgh: The Royal Scottish Museum
London: British Museum
Horniman Museum and Library
Victoria and Albert Museum
Oxford: Ashmolean Museum

INDIA
Bombay: Prince of Wales Museum of Western India
Calcutta: Indian Museum
Madras: Government Museum and National Art Gallery
New Delhi: National Museum of India

U.S.A.
Boston: Boston Museum of Fine Arts
Los Angeles: Los Angeles County Museum of Art
New York: Metropolitan Museum of Art

PAINTINGS FOR THE EAST INDIA COMPANY

Mildred Archer

1

Fig. 1 ***A family of Gaddis (shepherds)*** *of the Punjab Hills with a flock of goats and a sheep-dog by Huzuri, Kangra, c. 1900. The reduction of the goats to midget proportions is typical of the naive charm of Company painting. (Private Collection.)*

2

C. H. Cannings

Fig. 2 **Toddy-seller** *by Bani Lal (1850–1901), Patna,* c.*1870.*
A woman seller of liquor is pouring out drinks for two customers. The artist was an employee of the Patna painter, Shiva Lal, who had known Sir Charles D'Oyly and been greatly influenced by him. Shiva Lal specialised in Company paintings of occupations and castes.
(Private Collection.)

3

C. H. Cannings

Fig. 3 **Horse and groom** *by Shaikh Muhammad Amir, Company painter of Karraya, a suburb of Calcutta,* c.*1845.*
This picture is part of a set depicting the mansion, servants, carriages, horses and dogs of an unknown British resident of Calcutta. The name of this horse, Barrister, is inscribed on the reverse.
(Private Collection.)

4

C. H. Cannings

Created by local artists working for the European communities, Company paintings depict everyday life in India with great skill, charm and colour

'Company Painting' is a term which has come into use to describe the type of painting made in the eighteenth and nineteenth centuries by Indian artists working for the European communities in India. From the seventeenth century, East India companies from Holland, France, Denmark and England, as well as merchants from Portugal, were trading in India, but by the late eighteenth century it was the British who predominated. So well known was the English Company that it came to be nicknamed 'John Company'. At this time the nature of the community was changing. As the British extended their influence over India, the tough trader was gradually replaced by Company servants with more cultured interests – administrators, doctors, lawyers. Moreover, as life became less hazardous they were joined by women from the same social background.

A number of the British brought with them the interests and enthusiasms of their time, a desire to explore this new 'exotic' country, to look at its ancient buildings, its brilliant birds and flowers and its curious animals. They were intrigued by the people and everyday life around them, the complexity of the households with their many servants and the odd methods of transport – elephants, palanquins and peacock-boats. They were fascinated by the variety of costume denoting class, caste or race, the strange occupations which could be seen in every town or village and the bizarre festivals and gods.

5

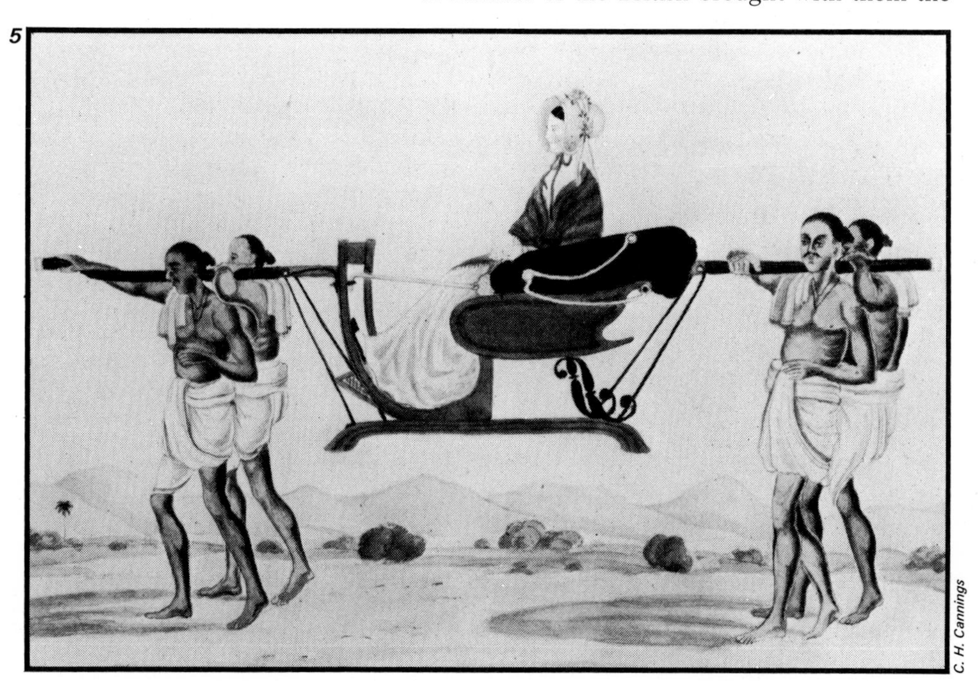

C. H. Cannings

Fig. 4 ***Sweetmeat- and fish-sellers**, probably by Jamuna Prasad (1859–84), Patna, c.1880. The bright colours and hard style are characteristic of an element in Patna painting which retained a strong Indian flavour. (Private Collection.)*

Fig. 5 ***English lady being carried in a 'tonjon'**, Cuttack, c.1840. This picture is part of a set similar to that illustrated in Figure 3. The group includes pictures of the servants, pets and conveyances of a British resident in Cuttack, the administrative headquarters of Orissa. (Private Collection.)*

Numerous journals and letters of the period record the delight of the newcomer in India. As Captain Mundy wrote: 'In the picturesque properties of the scene, how greatly does this Indian assemblage transcend our own! Instead of red, rectangular buildings, square doors, square windows, formal lines of booths, and, what is worse than all, the dark dingy dress of the figures . . . we have here domes, minarets, fanciful architecture, and a costume, above all, flaunting in colours, set off with weapons, and formed, from the easy flow of its drapery, to adorn beauty and disguise deformity . . . Every hut, equipage, utensil and beast of India is picturesque'.

It was only natural that the British in India should want a pictorial record of the scene which they could send home to their relatives in England or mount in their own scrapbooks to remind them, in their retirement, of the country which had afforded them so much delight. Those who could sketch made their own records, but not everyone was talented in this field and many looked for assistance to Indian artists.

The latter were quick to understand the needs of these new patrons. With the breakdown of the Mughal Empire, patronage from Indian rulers and gentry had greatly declined and many artists were looking for a new source of employment. Some took service with the East India Company itself and became draughtsmen assisting the military engineers with map-making, survey work or architectural projects. Some were privately employed by British men and women, but the majority began to produce pictures of costumes, occupations, servants, transport, festivals and gods which could be hawked around the British cantonments or sold in the bazaars.

Considerable adjustments had to be made by these Indian artists. Traditional Indian painting had little appeal to most Europeans, who were accustomed either to large-scale oil-painting or to the soft water-colour technique. Indian miniatures with their strange perspective, linear composition, gouache technique and brilliant colour struck the average Englishman as hard, dry, garish and distorted, as well as lacking in grace or realism. Efforts were made by the British to 'educate' Indian artists by showing them books of engravings or their own water-colour drawings. Indian artists have always been versatile and, just as under the Mughals they had absorbed Persian styles, so under the British they soon adjusted their technique to the Western fashion. The result was a type of painting which, with its use of water-colour and realistic detail, delighted the new patrons.

These developments quickly showed themselves in natural history drawings. In the late eighteenth century, many of the British were actively employed in collecting specimens of birds, animals, insects and plants in order to identify and classify them. Dried plants and skins were being despatched to learned institutions in England and it was essential that these should be accompanied by accurate drawings showing the plant or animal in its natural state.

Perhaps the greatest contribution in this field was made by Dr. Roxburgh, who, as Superintendent of the Calcutta Botanic Garden, trained a small team of Indian artists and despatched 2,500 drawings of plants to the Directors of the East India Company in London, keeping a duplicate set at the Calcutta Herbarium. These superb drawings show meticulous regard for the structure of the plant yet preserve an Indian feeling for strong design and rhythm. At the same time, a number of private patrons such as the Chief Justice, Sir Elijah Impey and his wife, and Marquis Wellesley, the Governor-General of India, built up their own vast private collections (Fig. 6). Many army officers and civilians, such as Nathaniel Middleton, Dr. Fleming and Major Rind, also assembled collections.

Paintings of costumes and occupations, especially made for the British, first appeared in south India during the last quarter of the eighteenth century. Madras was the most flourishing of the Presidency cities and the collapse of Indian patronage in Tanjore provided willing artists. Sets of pictures were produced showing a husband and wife standing side by side holding the implements of their trade – a cook holding a kettle and a chicken, his wife a fish; an oil-seller holding pots of oil, his wife a measure; a weaver with a piece of cloth, his wife reeling cotton thread. To these were added studies of picturesque characters such as dancing-girls and ascetics. In the earliest sets the figures are placed against a plain gouache background – blue, green or lemon yellow – with a band of tangled cloud at the top. In the later sets a landscape with palm trees and rolling clouds is added and the colour gradually changes to soft water-colour washes.

Offshoots from this school evolved at Trichinopoly, Srirangam and Pudukkottai where the painters specialised in making sets of small pictures on mica, illustrating not only trades but festivals and deities, and this type of painting persisted until the end of the nineteenth century. Another small school developed on the Malabar Coast.

Painters would record with elegance and authority an Englishman's house, servants, carriages, horses and pets

A similar development occurred in eastern India, perhaps a few years later, at Murshidabad, the capital of the Mughal governors of Bengal. Here a flourishing school of indigenous painting had existed, but, with the eclipse of the Nawabs, the artists sought patronage from the British. They, too, specialised in paintings of trades and occupations on both paper and mica, and the gouache technique quickly gave way to water-colour. The majority of Murshidabad pictures are characterised by sombre colouring, elongated figures, jagged drapery and heavy black borders.

In the early years of the nineteenth century, Calcutta rapidly developed and many artists from other centres sought patronage from its wealthy merchants or professionals living in their great Palladian mansions. A special type of Company painting evolved here where the artist would record the house of a particular Englishman, his staff of servants, his carriages, horses and pets. No better guide to the social history of the period exists than in the work of artists such as Shaikh Muhammad Amir of Karraya, whose sets of illustrations show the vast retinue of servants – gold- and silver-stick bearers, hookah- and parasol-bearers, wine-coolers, dog-boys, grooms (Fig. 3), punkah-pullers and the many valets and table-servants employed in a Company household. All are drawn with an air of elegance and authority. An offshoot of this style developed in Cuttack, capital of Orissa, and resulted in pictures of a similar, if more diluted, type (Fig. 5).

With the decline of Murshidabad as an administrative centre, some of its artist-families migrated to Patna in Bihar, the centre of the Company's trade in the rich Ganges valley. Here a number of artist-families established shops, hawking sets of 'occupations' round the British residential suburb of Bankipore and at the *ghats* (landing-stages) where the 'budgerows' (barges) tied up for the night. It was here also that Sir Charles D'Oyly, one of the most accomplished British amateur artists, lived from 1821 to 1833. He ran a lithographic press which published not only his own books but the drawings of his friends and neighbours. He trained a Patna artist to work the press, and there is little doubt that it was largely D'Oyly's influence which led certain Patna painters to develop a style which is strongly reminiscent of British aquatints (Fig. 2). At the same time, other Patna painters retained a more traditional style, employing brilliant colours and hard, clear-cut forms (Fig. 4).

An offshoot of Patna painting developed at Benares and the vogue for pictures of occupations moved steadily across the continent in the wake of the British. It reached Lucknow (Fig. 8), spread to western India, and after 1848 to the Punjab. At Amritsar and Lahore, artists made portraits of the former Sikh rulers in a Western style, and until the present century, descendants of artists in the Punjab Hills preserved the old technique and continued to depict occupations (Fig. 1).

At Delhi a special form of Company painting developed. It was not until 1803 that the British occupied the Mughal capital. Here traditions of indigenous Indian painting were still strong and a wealth of Mughal architecture existed on every side. For the British, the acquisition of Delhi was an intense experience. Here at last they were occupying the city of the Grand Mughal, whose splendour had become a myth in Europe. It was inevitable that they should want drawings of all these monuments, and within a few years Indian artists obliged.

By 1810 large architectural drawings in pen and ink and wash, strongly reminiscent of the Italian drawings brought back by many of the British from the Grand Tour, were being produced. At Delhi, the Red Fort, the Qutb Minar, the mausoleums of Humayun and Safdar Jang were popular subjects; at Agra, the Fort, the mausoleum of Itimad-ud-daula and, above all, the Taj Mahal were constantly depicted. Fatepur Sikri and Akbar's mausoleum at Sikandra (Fig. 7) were further popular subjects. Such pictures showed buildings in minute architectural detail.

By about 1815 to 1820 a second type of Delhi painting was being made with the monument set in a landscape. By the middle of the century such paintings gave way to similar pictures on ivory which retained the meticulous detail of the Indian miniature. Side by side with paintings of monuments, Delhi artists made portraits of the Emperor Akbar II, and later of Bahadur II, seated in durbar or riding in procession followed by their minions and the British Resident. They also enjoyed a flourishing trade in ivory miniature portraits which at times can scarcely be distinguished from the work of British artists.

The Company style forms the last phase of traditional Indian painting. With their hybrid technique, the pictures have a strange, naive charm, and, as the British Raj passes into history, they are deservedly appreciated as nostalgic memorials of this vanished age.

6

R. B. Fleming

Fig. 6 ***Pink lotus** by a Calcutta artist,* c.*1800.*
This drawing, with its careful botanical details, is part of a collection of 2,660 illustrations made for Marquis Wellesley while he was Governor-General of India from 1797 to 1805.
(India Office Library, London.)

Fig. 7 ***The entrance gateway to Akbar's mausoleum at Sikandra** by Latif, an Agra painter,* c.*1820.*
Latif had the reputation of being particularly skilled in the painting of Mughal architecture. His picture shows the gateway before it was repaired by the British.
(India Office Library.)

Fig. 8 ***Hookah-bearer**, Lucknow,* c.*1825-30.*
This is a part of a large set of pictures showing servants, trades, and castes. The hookah-bearer was an important member of the household.
(India Office Library.)

8

R. B. Fleming

7

R. B. Fleming

MUSEUMS AND COLLECTIONS

Examples of Company Painting may be seen at the following:

GREAT BRITAIN

London: British Museum
India Office Library
Victoria and Albert Museum

FURTHER READING

Indian Architecture and the British 1780–1830 by Mildred Archer, Feltham, 1968.
Indian Painting for the British, 1770–1880 by Mildred and W. G. Archer, London, 1955.
Twilight of the Mughals by Percival Spear, Cambridge, 1951.
Company Drawings in the India Office Library by Mildred Archer, London, now in preparation.

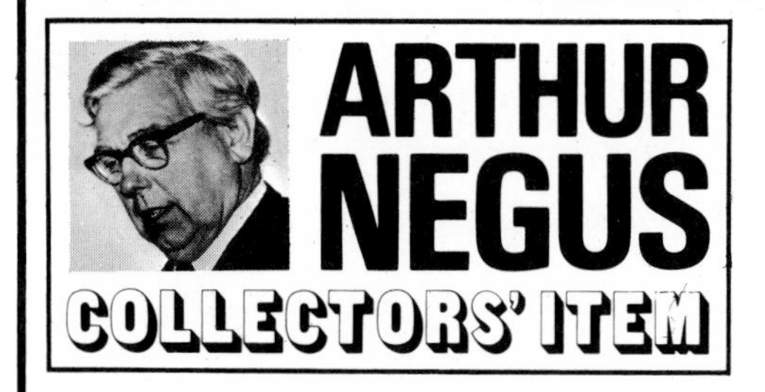

VISITING-CARD CASES

Sadly, in our modern world we no longer enjoy the small social courtesies which were so much a part of the Victorian era – such as the leaving of a card when one called to see a friend and found that he or she was out. Gone with this charming, if superfluous, custom are the equally delightful cases designed to carry these cards.

Cases were made and embellished in a great variety of materials – silver, polished wood, ivory, tortoise-shell, papier mâché or mother-of-pearl – all suitably decorative and attractive to suit the tastes of society ladies and gentlemen.

The earliest card cases were of silver and were made from about 1800 – the hallmarks solve the dating problem. Other cases are less easy to date. For example, most mother of pearl cases were made in the 1860s and 1870s but some are known to have been produced in the 1830s. Papier mâché cases with 'gem painting' (a picture panel painted under the glass and backed with pearl or silver foil which made it sparkle) date from the 1850s, as do cases in tooled leather, sometimes decorated with *petit point* needlework or with porcupine quills set in ebony, and tartan ware cases. These last are colourful examples of a popular Victorian craft. Centred around the Scottish towns of Kincardine and Ayr, craftsmen produced all kinds of wooden objects, including card cases which they decorated with paintings of the various clan tartans. There is no end to the variety of decoration of these highly attractive little bygones.

Although they vary enormously in style their size is fairly constant. Cases designed for ladies are usually four by three inches, and less than half an inch thick. Lined with velvet, they have either a sliding cover or one that is hinged along the narrow end of the case. They were designed to hold about half a dozen cards. Cases for gentlemen tend to be a little wider and are hinged down the long side so that they open like a purse. The inside might be divided into compartments (usually of silk) designed to hold up to a dozen cards.

Gentlemen's cases often have a silver shield on the front on which the owner could have his monogram engraved. The lady's version generally has a name strip running along the thin edge of the lid.

Collecting Hints

Look out for tortoise-shell cases studded with gold piqué (gold pin-heads formed into a decorative pattern set into the shell). They are quite rare and, even at the period in which they were made, were owned only by the cream of society. Also rare, but less valuable, are mourning cases, suitably sombre in ebony or onyx and decorated with ivory or silver inlay. Learn to distinguish ivory from bone inlay, for the former is much more valuable. Over the years, ivory will retain its creamy coloration whereas bone will become dull and grey in tone.

It is often difficult to distinguish between mother-of-pearl cases of the 1830s and mid-century or later ones. There is a test which can be applied if a sliver of the pearl has come away from the case, which tends to happen from time to time. Early slivers were hand-cut and are therefore thicker than the later paper-thin pieces.

Where To Buy

Card cases are found in small, general antique shops. The inveterate junk shop browser is the person who will come across these small treasures at the most reasonable prices.

Prices

Prices are not high. Sometimes one can be found for only a few shillings but generally mother of pearl, silver, and tortoise-shell cases fetch between £1 and £3, depending on the amount of work involved in the decoration. Mourning cases and those with gold piqué decoration will cost a little more.

R. Todd-White

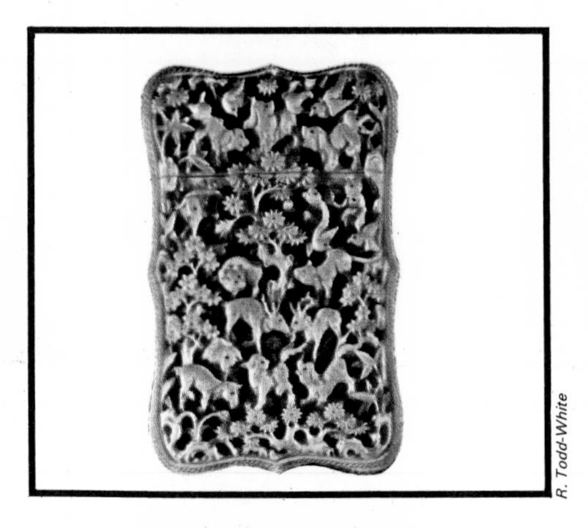
R. Todd-White

R. Todd-White

R. Todd-White

(far left) ***Ivory card case,*** *finely engraved with baboons and worth £18.*

(top left) ***Ivory card case*** *with deep-carved decoration of animals, costing £35.*

(bottom left) ***Silver card case*** *embossed with three winged cherubs, worth £11.*

(above) ***Ivory card case*** *with penwork scene of a farmer and his dog, priced at £14.*

Opposite: ***Papier mâche card case*** *with painted and mother-of-pearl flowers £8.*

(Maynard-Taylor Collection.)

Maynard-Taylor Collection — R. Todd-White

1

J. Freeman

2

J. Freeman

3

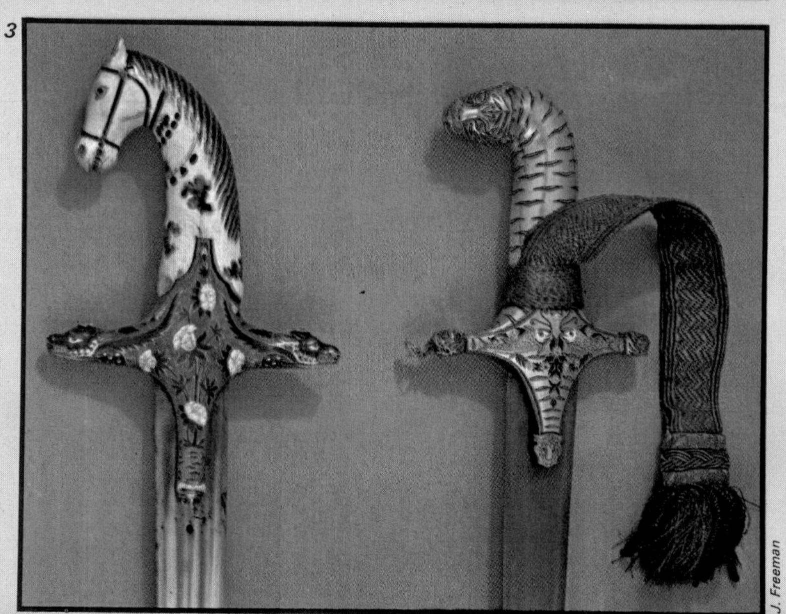

J. Freeman

4

J. Freeman

SWORDS & DAGGERS

Vesey Norman

Since Crusading times the glamour of the East has cast its spell over Westerners. The surviving inventories of the armouries of medieval castles sometimes list Saracen weapons. Archduke Ferdinand of Tyrol, the first of the great systematic collectors whose collection has survived, included in his Cabinet of Curiosities at Ambras not only the armours of contemporary captains and the crown of Montezuma, but also Japanese fans and armour and Persian robes. A few years later we find Rembrandt dressing his Biblical characters from his own collection of Orientalia, and among his sketches are several recording Mughal miniatures.

To the British, India has always had a peculiar fascination. Almost every county family has sent a son to 'shake the Pagoda tree' in the service of the East India Company, or to serve in one of the royal regiments which supported the Company's own armies on long-forgotten battlefields. This has meant that an enormous number of Indian weapons have found their way to Great Britain as souvenirs of a battle, as presentations, or as purchases.

It is only in the last few years that Indian arms have become the subject of systematic study. The conservatism of the Orient meant that development was exceptionally slow. Most of the surviving weapons are of the eighteenth century or later, and many show European influence in their decoration, and occasionally in their form; for instance, the adoption of the knuckle-guard is probably due to European influence. In the nineteenth century the influence of European designs on decoration is very noticeable, due not only to the native genius for copying, but also to conscious efforts by Europeans to 'improve' the work of local craftsmen by introducing them to Western designs.

The study of European arms is aided by portraits showing weapons in wear, but in India in the late periods the only large-scale paintings are those by visiting European artists, such as Tilly Kettle. Native miniatures are of little help because the scale makes it impossible to distinguish the subtle distinctions between the hilts from different areas, while repeated copying by miniaturists often makes such minute details unreliable. What Indian paintings do show, however, is that by the seventeenth century the distinction was often lost between the types of weapons of Muslim origin and those of Hindu origin. Miniatures frequently show princes and noblemen wearing a curved *tulwar* while holding in their hand the straight-bladed *khanda*, with its heavily guarded hilt. The former is of Muslim descent, the latter of Hindu.

Fig. 1 ***Three daggers.*** Left: *Probably made in Delhi, although of a Persian seventeenth-century type. The hilt of crystal set with rubies and emeralds in gold.* Centre: *A common type of civilian knife. The grip of jade set with precious stones, the scabbard mounts enamelled.* Right: *Probably Delhi work of the early seventeenth century. The gold hilt set with minute diamonds, rubies and emeralds, the scabbard a later replacement, but also of Delhi workmanship.*

Fig. 2 ***Two 'shamshir' hilts*** *with Persian watered-steel blades.* Left: *The hilt of* basse taille *enamel depicting stylised garden scenes deriving from Persian art. The colours suggest a Lucknow workshop, probably late eighteenth century.* Right: *Probably early nineteenth century. The gold enamelled with colours is associated with Jaipur.*

Fig. 3 Left: ***Straight-bladed sword (Firanghi).*** *The colours of the cross-guard suggest Delhi work of the first half of the nineteenth century. Gold grip, enamelled in imitation of a Mughal jade hilt.* Right: ***Gold-hilted 'shamshir'****, the painted enamel of a type found on Sindhi guns and on a sword presented by the Emir of Sind to George IV.*

Fig. 4 ***Mughal dagger*** *with carved jade hilt. The bridle of gold set with rubies. The pedestrian treatment of the head suggests eighteenth-century workmanship.*
(The above four plates by kind permission of the Trustees of the Wallace Collection, London.)

Embroidery of India

Christopher Cooke

1

Miki Slingsby

2

A. C. Cooper

3

A. C. Cooper

Based on ancient traditions and techniques, the embroidered textiles of India display a love of colour and a real understanding of shapes, symmetry and balance

Fine embroidery and magnificence in dress has long been valued in India. Stabo, writing in about 300 B.C. according to Megasthenes, 'talked of the Indian love for finery . . . worked in gold and ornamented with precious stones'; and he noted that they wore 'flowered garments of the finest muslin'. These could only have been embroidered, being too fine for paint or print.

Much later, when Akbar founded workshops (*kharkhanas*) at the end of the sixteenth century, the manufacture of all textiles, including carpets, was deliberately adjusted to court tastes and needs for the enhancement of the brilliant reputation of the Great Mughal. Much of the embroidery shows a typically Persian concern for overall pattern made up of delicately drawn sprays or bunches of flowers against a strongly laid-in background, often of gold thread or ribbed silks. Indigenous Indian taste, however, required a somewhat bolder delineation and colour as well as a more rhythmic treatment of the human figure, thus producing a more naturalistic and apparently spontaneous design, as well as the use of geometric patterns.

With the arrival of the European trading companies in the early seventeenth century, this tendency towards naturalism acquired a full-blown flavour reminiscent of Dutch flower-painting. Indeed, it would seem the Dutch attached great importance to the import of embroidered articles, the designs for which were often derived from popular religious engravings or from pattern-books sent out from Europe. At first the demand was often for material to make coverlets and bed-hangings decorated with overall sinuous patterning concerned with line and colour rather than with modelling and perspective (Figs. 9 and 10). Sometimes the same designs could be used for both embroidered and painted textiles (*chintzes*). It seems that the embroiderer was able to achieve a wider range of colour than the black, red and indigo of painted textiles. During the eighteenth century, European taste veered towards the more quixotic with its interest in *Chinoiserie*. Embroideries on dress-lengths made in Sind and the Punjab, and later shawls from Kashmir, were exported from India; of the latter the most sought after was the celebrated woven *pashmina*.

Throughout this period and until the present time, Indian people in many parts of the country have produced magnificent embroidery for themselves. Its production has reflected specific needs as well as unconscious descriptions of the circumstances of their personal lives. From the uses to which these embroidered pieces are put can be inferred the organisation of the community. The Punjabi grandmother begins working on a *bagh* with the birth of a child, while the sanctity of the home is enhanced by placing auspicious hangings on the walls and the bullocks' harness is decorated to underline the vital interdependence of man and beast. The usual coarse, cotton ground (*khaddar*) contrasts with the rich, glossy, floss silks of the overlay, indicating that labour is cheap but materials expensive. Local cotton is to hand in only a limited range of vegetable dyes, while the silk bought from peddling salesmen at the weekly market is obtainable in a far more brilliant range of colours. The work provides artistic training for children who may embark upon the creation of an article and produce a cogently worked design with little or no formal education. By following the examples of their tradition they learn the subtle relationships between colour, form, technique, shape and the effect of light and proportion, symmetry and overall balance in the design.

Artistic development in the almost self-sufficient village cultures may have been somewhat slow, but contact with the outside world was maintained as a result of the invaders from Central Asia and Europe who have always been attracted to the plains of Hindustan. It is significant that some of the best embroidery in the sub-continent is found in western India on the trade route between the Gangetic plain and the ports of Cambay, Diu and Surat (formerly Mughal, Portuguese and British establishments), all situated on the Gulf of Cambay. With one possible exception, all the stitches used in these embroideries are in common use the world over and, within India, similar design motifs are used in different areas. For example, the shape of the mango, oval with a pointed lobe set eccentrically, is echoed in the highly stylised pine-cone, or curled leaf (*kalka*) of Kashmir which is again reflected in the outline of drooping floral bouquets of Mughal architectural decoration.

For convenience, the different varieties of Indian embroidery may be put into eight groups: the work from the Vale of Kashmir, the *pulkharis* and *baghs* from the Punjab, the embroideries from Cutch, Kathiawar, Gujarat, Rajasthan and Sind, all of which areas are contiguous in western India. The celebrated *chaba rumals* come from the foothills of the Himalaya range. Three other types of embroidery quite unrelated are *Kasuti* from Mysore, *Chikankari* from Lucknow (Uttar Pradesh) and *Kantha* from Bengal. Another group is the work done by tribes living in remote areas either as nomads (the Bhils in Western India) in the upland jungle (the Banjaras in the Deccan) or on the hills (the Todas in the Nilgiris in the South and the Nagas along the mountainous north-east border of the country).

To many people Kashmiri work is summed up in the famous shawls, highly favoured by the Victorians, with their fine soft cloth made from the underfleece of the Tibetan goat, heavily decorated with woven borders and edges and deeply fringed. Unlike the other groups mentioned above, the manufacture of this shawl is and has been a strictly commercial undertaking, usually done by men.

The worked shawl itself was a later development, being a cheaper means of copying the extremely costly and sought-after woven item. This was in turn supplanted by the even cheaper article from Lyon and Paisley in the mid-nineteenth century. The patterning of the shawl is concentrated at each end of the piece (*pallu*) (Fig. 8) and is of an all-over texture worked in simple stem-, satin-, minute darning or herringbone-stitch. More delicate is embroidery which only shows on one side of the article (*aksi*), worked by splitting, with a fine needle, the warp thread, the top half of which is

Fig. 1 ***Toran (decoration over a door)**, Cutch, probably c.1900. Silk on cotton* (khaddar), *embroidered mainly in chain-stitch.*
The motifs embroidered on this complex and beautifully decorated piece include the sacred lotus and the green parrot, both indigenous to the Indian countryside.
(Author's Collection.)

Fig. 2 ***Pulkhari dress piece**, Hazara, Punjab, nineteenth century. White, green and yellow silk on a dark red cotton ground.*
(Victoria and Albert Museum, London.)

Fig. 3 ***Bagh shawl, cover or hanging** (detail), West Punjab, probably nineteenth century. The border of this fine example is of typical* bagh *design.*
(Victoria and Albert Museum.)

then picked up with a tiny darn stitch. The motifs used include drooping sprays of flowers and birds of brilliant plumage, all set in the swirling leaf-pattern shape, sometimes with human figures.

Almost as well known as the shawls are the cheap but serviceable floor carpets and rugs such as the *gabba* and *namda*. The latter is made up of a coarse mixed wool and cotton backing (*pattoo*), grey or cream-coloured. This is worked with large chain-stitch forming an outline to inserts of satin, cross-filling and couching stitches often all worked in wool. Solidly coloured areas may be filled by the chain-stitching radiating from the centre, or set in parallel lines very close together. The even cheaper *gabba* type of rug is basically *appliqué* and patch-work made up of old remnants.

Pulkharis and *baghs* are made all over the Punjab, but some of the best are produced around Rhotak by the Jats, a Hindu caste renowned for their expertise in agriculture and warfare. A handmade rough cotton forms the base material (*khaddar*), dyed dull red or indigo blue, on which

4

Museum Photo

the motifs are worked in untwisted floss silk giving a tapestry-like effect. The work is always done from the wrong side with the pattern emerging as the embroiderer works from one end of the cloth, guided only by the faint lines drawn by the silk thread. This accounts for the sometimes rather compressed design at the far end; deliberate mistakes or touches of black are introduced to ward off the evil eye. The stitches employed are usually the long and short darning, while double running is used to produce *chope* (pattern on both sides of cloth). These articles are purely domestic in use and their sale might only be effected in a financial crisis. The *chope*, begun at birth, is traditionally destined as a mother's gift to her daughter on marriage, as a symbol of maternal solicitude. A *pulkhari* proper (Fig. 2) is less heavily decorated, worked up in straight lines, for daily use in the house, while the magnificent *bagh* (Fig. 3) supports motifs so worked as to cover the whole ground. Here the pattern may be in straight rows or be a motif-strewn panel with a rich surrounding border. The design allows full play for the long threads which, worked horizontally, vertically and diagonally, catch the light with different intensity. The colours of the silk are basically golden yellow with purple, green, orange, dull red and, in the most spectacular examples, white.

Western India consists largely of semi-arid landscape dotted with scrub and the odd, symmetrically shaped, dark green wild mango tree. By contrast and as if in compensation, the embroidery of this area is richly coloured and sparkles with mirror-work (*shishidar*). The pieces are worked by the women and are used to decorate the house. The square (*chakla*) or rectangular (*chandrawa*) hanging is fixed to the wall, while the *toran* hangs over the lintel of the door and the *ordhni* covers seats and beds. The women also decorate their own bodices (*cholis*) and skirts (*ghagras*) as well as the harness and trappings of the family bullocks.

While all use the same coarse *khaddar* below and silk thread above, the embroidery from Cutch is generally of a particularly refined yet bold quality using natural motifs, the full-headed flower, continuous undulating floral sprays as borders or roundly profiled animals and birds, principally the peacock and green parrot, the latter a symbol of love (Fig. 1). These figures are worked in chain-stitch in subtly graduated colours to indicate modelling. Laid, couching and herring-bone-stiches are also used to outline the borders.

Below Cutch, in Kathiawar, the embroidery is rather more lively in character in that the ground is seen as part of the total pattern with the over-work. The appearance of each item is determined by different types of embroidery. The *heer bharat* is usually done on a dark crimson or indigo, but sometimes white, ground, worked in crimson silks with touches of green, yellow and black in geometric shapes making up a central panel. The central panel of the *chakla* (Fig. 5) often consists of a series of diagonally crossed squares of satin stitch worked in different directions centred with a mirror piece. Round this panel is often fitted a border made up of triangular pieces of black, blue or red remnants. *Abha bharat* makes more frequent use of inset mirrors with perhaps a wider colour range including light green, and pink on a yellow ground (Fig. 6). The mirror inset acts as the basis of the design (rather than as an adjunct) and can in some modern work, become its principle physical element.

In Sind the character of the embroidery is larger in scale, the *ordhni* being often several feet square in area and darkly opulent in tones of red and blue. The pattern arrangement is rather like a carpet, with roundels or lozenges inset with mirrors and small tassels while the ground is strewn with small motifs. At each end is a wide border decorated with upright flower plants at intervals, similar to dados in Mughal palaces (Fig. 7). A particular stitch giving character to Sindhi work is the *Sindhi taropa*, used extensively in Baluchistan on clothing. This consists of long thread stitches worked into the ground which are then looped up by other threads.

Other examples from this part of India are the appliqué work from Ahmedabad in Gujarat and

Fig. 4 **Rumal,** *Chamba, nineteenth century. Double satin-stitch in silk on both sides of the coarse muslin ground. This charming cloth depicts Krishna dancing with the milkmaids. It was used to cover gifts from the bride's family to that of the groom. (Victoria and Albert Museum.)*

Fig. 5 **Chakla wall decoration,** *Kathiawar, probably early twentieth century. Silk on indigo cotton with appliqué border. Worked in satin-stitch running horizontally and vertically, this is a fine example of* heer bharat *embroidery. (Author's Collection.)*

Fig. 6 **Panel,** *possibly part of a decoration for a bullock's harness, Kathiawar, early twentieth century. Silk on cotton with mirror insets. This example of* abha bharat *embroidery depicts Ganesh, the elephant-headed god of good fortune, with attendants, peacocks and the sacred umbrella. (Author's Collection.)*

Fig. 7 **Ordhni large coverlet,** *Sind, West Pakistan, second half of the nineteenth century. Chain-, flat- and cretan-stitches in red silk on shot plum and black silk. (Embroiderers' Guild, London.)*

Fig. 8 **Pashmina shawl,** *showing the embroidered end design* (pallu)*, Kashmir, c.1830. Loom embroidered with coloured wools and silks in various stitches. Scenes are framed by the characteristic curled leaf pattern called* kalka*. (Victoria and Albert Museum.)*

Fig. 9 **Angel motif** *from a bedspread, Cambay, Gujarat, late sixteenth or early seventeenth century. Very fine chain-stitch in silk on cotton. (Hardwick Hall, Derbyshire.)*

5

Miki Slingsby

6

Miki Slingsby

7

R. Todd-White

8

A. C. Cooper

9

C. M. Dixon

Kathtawar beadwork. The former describes the artefact exactly in that the pattern is built up of successive layers of cloth, covering or exposing the layers below as required. Colours are mainly confined to dull reds, creams and black.

In the beadwork the ground as well as motifs are worked in coloured beads, presenting similar overall patterns to other kinds of embroidery, but featuring animals rather than flowers. Beadwork is also used for the ring-shaped head-pad (*indhoni*) on which women traditionally rest their water-pots, and those delightful hanging objects made up of a series of quasi pincushions from which little birds, also made of beads, are suspended. Rajasthan is noted for its embroidery on leather, particularly saddlery and shoes (*jutis*) often with gold and silver thread. In the past were made knucklepads for shields showing scenes of court life which are very closely linked to the well-known local schools of miniature painting.

The treatment of the *chamba rumal* is very closely derived from the Pahari school of painting fostered by the rajahs of the small hill states of Kangra, Bilaspur, Mandi as well as Chamba. *Rumal* means a scarf or kerchief worn by the women which they decorate in a manner similar to that on their bodices and skirts. The *rumal* traditionally was sent to a bridegroom as an indication of his future wife's domestic skill. The embroidery is worked on a coarse muslin in simplified outline with the design often representing lyrical episodes in the life of Krishna the divine cowherd. The subject is treated in areas of solid colour in double satin-stitch on both sides of the cloth. A black silk outline is often added, while the whole might be trimmed with silver wire, particularly at the hems or to indicate jewellery on the figures (Fig. 4).

Kasuti work comes from the central Deccan and again is confined to personal effects belonging to the women. The motifs, on the usual *khaddar* ground (often indigo, black and white) are worked in cross-stitch (*menthi*) double-running stitch (*gaouti*) for outlining and filling large areas and a zigzag running stitch (*murgai*). The motifs are often objects of religious significance such as the South Indian Temple gateway (*gopuram*), the temple chariots which house the sacred image on its journey around the countryside (*ratha*), the sacred Tulsi plant, a symbol of the hearth, or the bull sacred to Shiva. Lucknow *chikankari* is white embroidery on fine white muslin and is much used for the decoration of the necks to the *kurta* (man's long shirt) and on the ends of saris. The stitches are complicated; mainly used are the *bukhra*, an inverted satin-stitch which is formed into knots, *katao* which is minuscule appliqué work and *kalai*, a very fine buttonhole which produces one of the embroidery's chief characteristics, the open fret. (Fig. 11). The Kanthas of Bengal, are based on an old tradition recently resurrected, of white embroidery sewn on to several layers of white or yellow silk to form quilting. These used to be much sought after by the merchants of the East India Company. The stitch used is the common running stitch with coloured thread sometimes introduced in the borders. The composition of the panel often has the sacred lotus as a central motif, a tree of life in each of the four corners and an undulating floral spray border.

The facts that these embroidered articles are still much used, the often extreme climate, and the economic circumstances of most Indian families, do not encourage the survival of very old work. The collector is therefore unlikely to find many old pieces in good condition, but will find plenty of material of more recent date in Britain as well as in India.

10

Museum Photo

11

A. C. Cooper

Fig. 10 ***Detail of a hanging*** *from the East India Company import trade, Gujarat, c.1680. Very fine chain-stitch in silk on cotton. (Victoria and Albert Museum.)*

Fig. 11 ***Detail of a Chikankari handkerchief,*** *Dacca, nineteenth century. Various stitches in silk and cotton on fine muslin. (Victoria and Albert Museum.)*

MUSEUMS AND COLLECTIONS

Indian textiles may be seen at the following:

GREAT BRITAIN

London: Embroiderers' Guild
Victoria and Albert Museum

INDIA

Ahmedabad: Calico Museum of Textiles

FURTHER READING

Embroideries from the Permanent Collection – The Embroiderers' Guild, introduction to the catalogue by J. L. Nevinson, London, 1971.

Origins of Chintz with a Catalogue of Indo-European Cotton Paintings in the Victoria and Albert Museum by John Irwin and K. Brett, London, 1970.

Journal of Indian Textile History, a Calico Museum of Textiles publication, Ahmedabad, 1955–67.

The Romance of Indian Embroidery by Kamala S. Dongerkery, Bombay, 1951.

Desmond Guinness

THE IRISH COUNTRY HOUSE

1

Fig. 1 **Westport House,** *Westport, Co. Mayo, Eire, by Richard Castle, c.1731. Seen from the south east. Home of the Marquess of Sligo, this magnificent house was designed by a then unknown German architect, Richard Castle. Later, until his death in 1751, Castle was to enjoy the principal country house practice in Ireland. It is said that, if he was not satisfied with the way a building was going, he would make the workmen pull it all down and start again. His massive, Palladian stone piles might have encouraged their owners in the mistaken belief that theirs was a stable, permanent society.*

2

Fig. 2 **Four Courts,** *Dublin, Eire, by James Gandon (1742–1824), late eighteenth century. Seen from the River Liffey.*
Although English, James Gandon was one of the few truly professional architects of Ireland in the eighteenth century. After the arrival of Palladianism in about 1720, a large number of houses were put up by builders following their own or their client's whim. Houses created in this way have great charm and individuality, but lack the strict adherence to classical detail and proportion felt to be necessary for aesthetic correctness.

3

Author's Photo

4

Transglobe

Irish country houses share the grace and beauty of classical Georgian architecture with the charm and individuality of the owners' personal whims

Very little architecture survives in Ireland dating from Elizabethan or Jacobean times. Owing to the unsettled state of the country, the castle stronghold continued in use for a hundred years longer than in England. A great spate of house-building, however, followed the Battle of the Boyne (1690) which ushered in a hundred years of peace and relative prosperity. So it was that in Ireland the classical house developed straight from the castle.

At first these houses were modest in size, of red brick with tall chimneys and sash windows reminiscent of the Dutch houses from which they derive. By 1720, however, the Palladian invasion had arrived, and true classical correctness reached Ireland for the first time. From then on, the Georgian house can be divided into two categories – firstly those designed by an architect and therefore of correct proportions, and secondly those put up by some builder, following his own or his client's whim or fancy, where, as often as not, there is as little correctness in the detail and disposition of the classical motifs as there was in the Tudor houses of England.

Much of the charm and individuality of the Irish country house derives from these amateurish creations. There is a certain awkwardness about them which gives them a distinctive flavour. Everything goes into the façade – the sides and back are a medley of misplaced windows and ugly drainpipes. James Gandon, a truly professional architect, who designed Dublin's Customs House and Four Courts, despised the amateur. 'But no sooner do these lads obtain a smattering in drawing', he wrote, 'but they think themselves qualified for Architects; and many Gentlemen who assume pretensions to taste in design and economy give their scrawls to these tyros to make what they call drawings, which are afterwards produced over a bottle as their own. From these joint productions are the many medleys of country houses derived which are scattered about to the disgrace of the taste of the country'.

One of the greatest houses in Ireland, Castletown, Celbridge, was begun in 1722 for Speaker Conolly. The architect was an Italian, Allessandro Galilei, who is best known for having designed the façade of St. John in Lateran, Rome, thought by many to be second only to St. Peter's itself. Percival wrote to Bishop Berkeley who was advising Conolly on the building of the house: 'You will do well to recommend to him the making use of all the marbles he can get of the production of Ireland for his chimneys, for since this house will be the finest Ireland ever saw, and by your description fit for a Prince, I would have it as it were the epitome of the Kingdom, and all the natural rarities she afford

5

The Green Studio

6

The Green Studio

7

Author's Photo

Fig. 3 ***Castletown House,*** *Celbridge, Co. Kildare, Eire, by Alessandro Galilei (1691–1737), begun 1722. Thought to be the finest Georgian house in Ireland, Castletown was built for the Conolly family. Its Italian designer, Galilei, came to Ireland in 1714, and later built the famous façade of St. John in Lateran, Rome. His design for Castletown set a much-used pattern for country houses with a central block linked by curved colonnades to the two wings.*

Fig. 4 ***Castlecoole,*** *Enniskillen, Co. Fermanagh, Northern Ireland, by James Wyatt, 1795. The most perfect neo-classical house in Ireland, Castlecoole is decorated with plasterwork by Joseph Rose, one of the greatest stuccodores.*

Fig. 5 ***Leinster House,*** *Kildare Street, Dublin, Eire, by Richard Castle, 1745, for the Earl of Kildare; it was called Kildare House until 1766 when Kildare was created Duke of Leinster. Engraving from Rocque's* Map of Dublin, *1756. In his* Views of the City of Dublin, *Malton described this fine house as 'the most stately private edifice in the city, . . . enjoying in the tumult of a noisy metropolis all the retirement of the country'.*

Fig. 6 ***Bellinter House,*** *Co. Meath, Eire, by Richard Castle, c.1750. Engraved by F. R. Hay, drawn and published by J. P. Neale, London, 1820. Like Castlecoole, this fine building follows the basic plan devised by Galilei for Castletown, the roofed passages taking the place of his colonnades.*

Fig. 7 ***Mount Ievers Court,*** *Sixmilebridge, Co. Clare, Eire, 1732. The stone façade. Still in the possession of the Ievers family, this fine house appears to date from about 1710, an example of the time-lag between Irish and European architecture.*

should have a place there. I would examine the several woods there for inlaying my floors, and wainscot with our own oak, and walnut: my stone stairs should be of black palmers' stone, and my buffet adorned with the choicest shells our strand afford. I would even carry my zeal to things of art: my hangings, bed, cabinets and other furniture should be Irish, and the very silver that ornamented my locks and grates should be the produce of our mines. But I forget that I write to the gentleman of the country who knows better what is proper and what the Kindgom affords'.

The design of Castletown set a pattern that was repeated over and over again in both large and small houses. The central block is linked by curved colonnades to wings which stretch forth in an eternal gesture of welcome to greet the visitor. An early visitor to Castletown admired the 'cloisters'; classical colonnades were then of course unknown in Ireland. The simpler houses had to make do with curved sweeps or curtain walls instead, but in every case utilitarian yards were formed behind the wings, which were really part of the farm – life in Ireland has always been closely linked to the soil.

This arrangement of house and outbuildings has been termed 'the economic Palladian layout', and is Ireland's greatest single contribution to country house design. Its popularity has been explained in several ways. Some say that as no buildings existed on the land previously, it was a convenient solution. Others insist that the pretensions of the Anglo-Irish demanded the longest possible façade, so that all sorts of buildings and outhouses were pressed into service to provide one. Again, it has been suggested that the bawn (fortified enclosure) which surrounded castle strongholds so lately abandoned was used as an enclosure for cattle, and that for reasons of security the animals were kept near at hand, instead of in a yard some distance away, as would have been the case in England.

A German architect, Richard Castle, arrived in Ireland in 1728 and stayed there until his death in 1751. He was a true perfectionist, and it is said that if he was not pleased with the way a building was progressing, he would make the workmen pull it down and start again. He is credited with having built no fewer than twenty-eight country houses, of which Powerscourt, Westport and Russborough are the most famous. In Dublin he built Leinster House, Tyrone House and Clanwilliam House (85 St. Stephen's Green), as well as the Dining Hall and Printing House in Trinity College.

Builders' pattern books contained detailed measurements and instructions for every kind of exterior and interior detail

Richard Castle's houses are massive, Palladian, stone piles which seem as much at home in the green Irish landscape as on the dusty, flat plain of the Veneto. There is a certain heaviness in their proportions which might have encouraged their owners in the mistaken belief that theirs was a stable, permanent society. There were many builders' pattern books available at that time, and from the lists of subscribers given in them, it is clear that they found their way to Ireland. They contained detailed measurements and instructions for builders, not only for the house itself, but including every kind of interior detail such as the panelling, mantelpieces, window surrounds, staircases, plaster ceilings and so on.

As the eighteenth century progressed two tendencies made themselves apparent. The first was the time-lag whereby fashions were slow to change and old styles were practised long after they had been abandoned elsewhere; the second was the up-to-the-minute taste of leaders of European fashion such as the Earl of Charlemont. He was abreast if not ahead of contemporary trends and introduced neo-classical architecture to Ireland as early as 1758 when he built the Marino Casino, an exquisite temple at Clontarf, Dublin.

Irish houses are often all of a piece, and did not develop in a variety of styles as they did in England, where alteration and addition by succeeding generations are the rule rather than the exception. The fact that money often ran low after the Act of Union in 1801 may account for the relatively high proportion of houses that escaped nineteenth-century 'improvements'.

The plasterwork in Irish houses is sometimes of exceptionally high quality. There is a deep-rooted belief that all such decoration was the work of Italian craftsmen. It is true that three Italians did come, the Francini brothers and Cramillion, and that they had an important influence on the Irish stuccodores by teaching them new techniques and introducing the human figure to plaster decoration for the first time. But there are hundreds of Irish names to be found on the rolls of the Guilds of Plasterers, which functioned in Cork and Limerick as well as in Dublin, not to mention the Catholics and other dissidents who were barred from official practice of the craft on sectarian grounds.

Irish Rococo reached its high-water mark about 1750; birds, flowers and musical instruments mingle in a profusion of rococo gaiety. The style prevailed until the neo-classical decoration, which made extensive use of repetitive moulds and plaques, became fashionable towards the end of the eighteenth century and brought an end to freehand artistry.

English travellers in the Georgian era did not hold our country houses in high esteem. 'In most cases these houses maintain no *culture* worth speaking of, nothing but an insidious bonhomie, an obsolete bravado, and a way with horses', writes one. And again: 'Fine house and everything in perfect style, but whether from prejudice or not I fancied there was a *parvenu* air in all around – English stiffness grafted on to Irish good nature' Certainly the furniture and art objects in Irish houses have never been able to rival those in England – wooden family portraits stare fixedly at each other across the front hall, keeping company with an Irish elk and an assortment of boots, fishing rods and so on. Books by the yard, bought for their bindings rather than for their content, fill the library, but just the same the silver, glass and furniture of the period is now avidly sought.

The mock castle began to be built in about 1800 with pepper-pot turrets, arrow-slits and battlements, conjuring up visions of 'the rust of the Baron's wars'. The wheel had come full circle, and after a hundred years the castle was once more in fashion.

The changeover started with Castle Ward. This extraordinary house was built by an unknown architect for Mr. Bernard and Lady Anne Ward in 1762. The story goes that they could not agree on the style of their new house – Mr. Ward wanted a classical house and his wife one in the gothic taste after Walpole's Strawberry Hill in England. The result was a compromise – a house that is classical in front and gothic at the back.

8

Author's Photo

Fig. 8 ***The Marino Casino,*** *Clontarf, Dublin, Eire, built by Sir William Chambers, 1758, for the Earl of Charlemont. Engraving.*
Irish taste was exposed to current fashions in the eighteenth century by such leaders of European taste as the Earl of Charlemont. He kept abreast of contemporary trends and introduced neo-classical architecture to Ireland with the building of this exquisite temple as early as 1758.

Figs. 9 and 10 ***Castle Ward,*** *Strangford, Co. Down, Northern Ireland, built by an unknown architect in 1762 for Mr. Bernard and Lady Anne Ward.*
Built by a husband and wife with opposing tastes, this house is a living reminder of a remarkable compromise. Lady Anne wanted her house built in the gothic taste after Walpole's Strawberry Hill, while Mr. Ward wanted his strictly classical. The result was a house with two faces: gothic on the north side or back (Fig. 9), and classical on the south or front (Fig. 10).

9

Transglobe

10

Transglobe

WHERE TO SEE IRISH COUNTRY HOUSES

EIRE
Bantry House, Bantry, Co. Cork.
Open Monday to Friday in summer.
Carton, Maynooth, Co. Kildare.
Open Sunday and Monday in summer.
Castletown, Celbridge, Co. Kildare. Open Sundays, and daily except Tuesdays in summer.
Marino Casino, Clontarf, Dublin.
Key available on request.
Powerscourt House, Enniskerry, Co. Wicklow.
The grounds open daily in summer.
Westport House, Westport, Co. Mayo.
Open daily in summer.

NORTHERN IRELAND
Castlecoole, Enniskillen, Co. Fermanagh.
Open daily in summer.
Castle Ward, Strangford, Co. Down. Open daily except Monday in summer. The grounds open daily throughout the year.

ARTHUR NEGUS
COLLECTORS' ITEM

TINSEL PICTURES

Tinsel pictures are among the most transitory of nineteenth-century gewgaws. Beginning in the late 1820s, and disappearing from view in the 1850s, they were very popular in the intervening twenty years. Linked closely with the resurgent theatre, they depict some of the famous actors of the day in the roles that made them famous. The popular stage was often referred to as the 'gaudy', and these pictures reflect that taste exactly. Mr. Dale as Claude Amboine in 'Ruth – Or the Lass that Loves a Sailor' was a universal favourite, as was Mr. Horn in the role of the dreaded outlaw 'Caspar'. As well as theatrical personalities, there was a brief fashion for tinsels of the Queen at the time of her Coronation in 1837, and other notable figures of the day. These representations always conformed to the one pattern: a heroic posture against a plain background of trees, a curtain, or the sea. All the embellishment went with the figure, and none at all into the setting; thus, technique helped to give the pictures the dramatic quality demanded by the public, and provided a useful medium for advertising plays and leading players. Tinsels were displayed prominently in taverns and coffee houses, together with play-bills and cartoons, and helped to enliven the often gloomy interiors of the era before flaming gas lamps and coloured glass were introduced.

Above right ***Miss Waylett as Apollo*** *in 'Midas', 1832. £20.*
Below left ***Mr. Collins as Ivanhoe*** *in 'The Maid of Judah', published by Skelt. £35.*
Below right ***Neptune,*** *published by A. Park. £35.*

Opposite: ***Edward, the Black Prince.*** *£35.*

Collecting Hints

A large number of fakes have been produced in recent years – most of them drawn from figures from the theatrical souvenirs produced in the early eighteenth century for Pollock's famous shop and toy museum in Monmouth Street. The quality of paper used is generally a sure guide.

Prices

Single pictures sell for anything up to seven or eight pounds in good condition, and pairs for roughly double that sum.

Park Antiques, London: K. Hoddle

Park Antiques, London: K. Hoddle

Irish Interiors and Furniture

The Knight of Glin

From the early seventeenth century, the castles of Ireland began to be furnished and decorated in a magnificent and opulent fashion

1

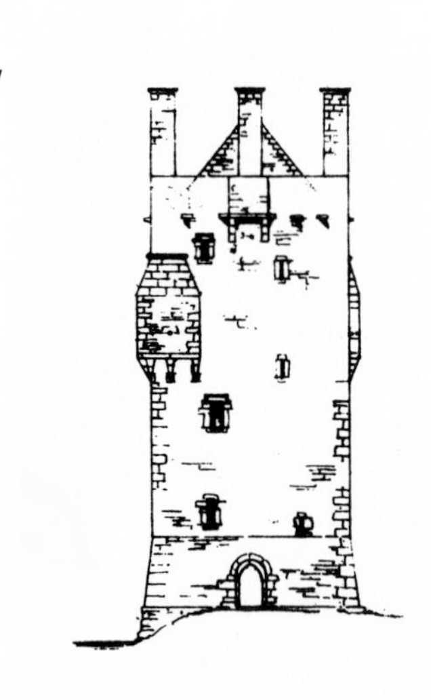

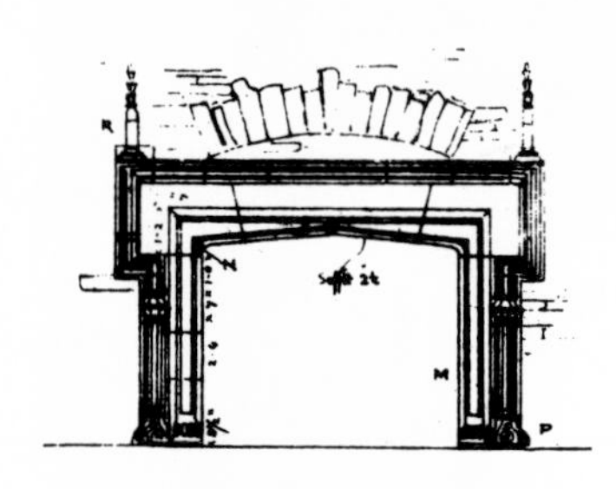

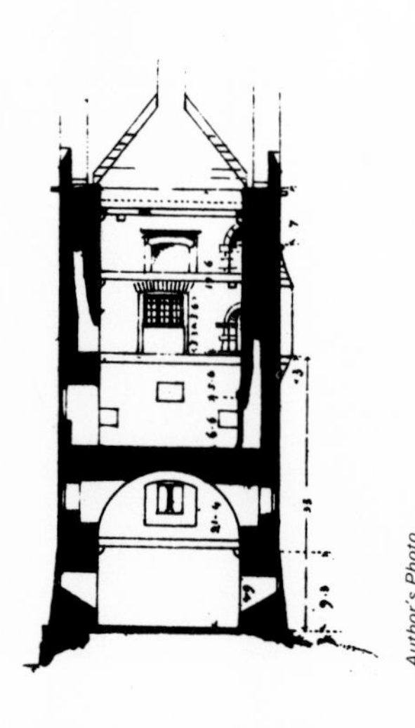

Author's Photo

In medieval Ireland the leading Gaelic and Anglo-Irish chieftains and barons owned vast tracts of forest, bog and grazing land, among which stood the great walled castles such as Trim, Liscarroll, Askeaton or Roscommon. These are real 'castles' in the English sense of the word but below them in the feudal hierarchy ranked the smaller tower houses of the cadet branches of the great Norman families and lesser Irish chieftains. There are literally thousands of these towers all over the country and, owing to the bloody wars and massacres that echoed over the lands and battlements of Ireland, castle-building carried on until the middle of the seventeenth century.

Ireland possesses no sixteenth-century 'prodigy' houses and, as an English traveller noted in 1762, into the bawns, or courtyards, of these habitations of the old gentry, 'they nightly drove their whole stock of Cattle for security against their rieteous Neighbours'. Owen Brereton went on to note that these castles 'are all built very high but take up little Room, Almost All of them resemble a very large Tower Steeple of a Church . . .'. The elevations, details and plans of such a tower house (Fig. 1), by the brilliant English Victorian architect E. W. Godwin, show that the living quarters were on the upper floors and the finest chimney-pieces on the third. The furnishings of these rooms must have been simple in the extreme. Luke Gernon in 1620 exclaims 'when you come to your chamber do not expect a canopy and curtaynes', and another admittedly biased writer in the late sixteenth century, after having stated that 'the wild Irish' had no candles on their tables, went on to say, 'what do I speak of tables? Indeed, they have no

2

Museum Photo

Fig. 1 ***Fantstown,*** *Co. Limerick, drawings by the architect E. W. Godwin, c.1860. (Victoria and Albert Museum, London.)*

Fig. 2 ***Double-ramped staircase*** *from Eyre Court Castle, Co. Galway, Irish, c.1670. Carved oak. (Detroit Institute of Arts, Michigan.)*

Fig. 3 ***Fiddle-back, balloon-seated chair,*** *Irish, c.1740–50. Mahogany. (David Stockwell, Wilmington, Del.)*

Fig. 4 ***The entrance hall,*** *now the Music Room, Castle Ward, Co. Down. The plasterwork is typically Irish.*

tables, but set their meat upon a bundle of grass and use the same grass as napkins to wipe their hands'. Later he bewails the lack of sheets and feather beds in the tower houses of these country chieftains. In reality they would probably have had benches, chests and a high table in the great hall. This was often constructed of mud and thatch and stood at one end of the tower inside the walls of the bawn, but owing to its impermanent nature none of these has survived.

This feudal life continued in the wilder parts of Ireland well into the middle of the eighteenth century, for Edward Willes, Lord Chief Baron of the Irish Exchequer, was told by Michael Cuff of Ballinrobe, in about 1753 (a man who was still living in what was then 'the most perfect and complete Bawne in Ireland'), that he had some friends who had gone on a fishing expedition on Lough Corrib and landed to have an alfresco picnic of freshly caught broiled fish. Willes tells an interesting tale of an invitation from a local clan chieftain, possibly one of the Joyces, to his house, '. . . a Magnificent palace, where . . . there were two long Cabins Thatched opposite to one another, the one was the Kitchen and apartments for the family, the other was the Entertaining room, neatly strewed according to the Irish Fashion with Rushes and the upper End of the Room was a kind of Platform raised above the ground with Boards and two or three Blankets one each which was the Lodging for strangers and visitors. A bottle of Brandy was the whet before dinner, and the entertainment was a Half Sheep Boiled top, Half Sheep roasted at Bottom, broiled Fish on one side, a great wooden bowl of Potatoes on the other, and a heaped plate of salt in the middle. After dinner pretty good claret, and an enormous Bowl of Brandy Punch which according to the old as well as the Modern Irish Hospitality, the guests were pressed to take their full share of . . .'. The visiting servants were given a bottle of brandy each and later in the evening 'when the Chief began to grow mellow, he Call'd his Favourite Girl to sing, which she did very well and was a neat handsome jolly girl. Before he called her in, he stipulated with his guests that they were welcome to any liberty with her from the Girdle upwards but he would not permit any underhand doings'. Later a bagpiper and a bard sang about the glorious deeds of the Chief's illustrious and warlike ancestors. At last the visitors were allowed to go to bed but the next morning, after a breakfast consisting of another bowl of punch, they

3

Author's Photo

4

Author's Photo

5

Edwin Smith

6

Author's Photo

7

Fig. 5 ***The saloon,*** *Castlecoole, Co. Fermanagh, by James Wyatt, 1795; the plasterwork by Joseph Rose of London.*

Fig. 6 ***Small cabinet on stand,*** *Irish,* c.*1720–30. (Miss Crosbie Collection, Malahide, Dublin.)*

8

Author's Photo

Fig. 7 ***The Library*** *at Ballyfin House, Co. Leix, by Sir Richard Morrison. Watercolour by the Marquis de Massigny de la Pierre,* c.*1860. (Admiral Sir John Coote, Bt., Collection.)*

Fig. 8 ***The drawing room*** *at Bellevue, Co. Wicklow. Drawing by Anne Maria La Touche, 1841. The plasterwork, probably by the Dublin stuccodore Michael Stapleton, is in the Adam/Wyatt manner. (C. J. La Touche Collection.)*

Fig. 9 ***Card-table,*** *Irish,* c.*1750. Carved mahogany. This table shows the flat, rounded-off carving typical of Irish work, as well as square paw feet and carved legs. (Private Collection.)*

Fig. 10 ***Bottle-stand,*** *Irish,* c.*1740. Carved mahogany. This uniquely Irish stand points to the well-known proclivity of the Irish for over-indulgence in the pleasures of Bacchus. Note also the typical trifid feet. (Stair and Co., London.)*

9

Author's Photo

10

Author's Photo

had the greatest difficulty leaving. A case of too much and too little hospitality!

To return to the seventeenth century, signs of more sophisticated taste are documented in the extensive correspondence of Richard Boyle, the first and 'great' Earl of Cork. He was importing 'plancks of walnut tree' from France as early as 1613 and four years later he sent bedsteads from Bristol to his 'new house at Lismoor'. Tapestries, state beds and elaborately upholstered chairs, stools, many with 'ffryndges of Crymson Silck and silver' frequently occur in his accounts. Some of these were imported from Edward Spence of London, 'Upholsterer dwelling at the sign of the grasshopper', but mention is also made of 'the joyner of the Chapple Isolde (Chapel Isod near Dublin) supplying 'my Rownd table' and Thomas Smyth of Dublin made up his 'red velvett chayre, stools and long cushions'. Lord Cork was also given presents (possibly bribes) by his neighbours, for instance: 'my good friend Mrs. Nicholas Wice (Wyse) of Waterford's wife' presented him with a 'faier lardg ebbony cabbynet or case of boxes'. This is probably an Augsburg piece imported into Ireland earlier than 1624. Other contemporary inventories prove that great nobles like the Earl of Kildare had the most elaborate furnishings in their castles and the inventory of Maynooth shows the rooms hung with tapestries and furnished with highly decorative pieces. Even as far away as Co. Limerick, Sir Hardress Waller of Castletown Waller decorated his newly acquired castle with carpets, tapestry hangings, curtains, cushioned chairs and couches.

Unfortunately, this new-found opulence was either burnt or pillaged in the ensuing Cromwellian wars and it is not until the quarter-century between 1660 and 1685 that such peaceful activities as painting and the cultivation of the polite arts could again be indulged. By this period the Elizabethan and Cromwellian settlers, the 'old English' and those Irish chieftains that conformed to the Protestant faith began to move out of their castles and tower houses and started building the first country houses as we know them. Very few have survived but a glance at the elaborate double staircase originally at Eyre Court Castle, County Galway (Fig. 2), shows that Ireland was not without its fine carvers and artisans at this period.

Under the viceroyalty of the Duke of Ormond, guilds were formed in Dublin. The contemporary inventories of his own chief residence, Kilkenny Castle, list silver mirrors, tables and candle stands, 'a chrystall Shambiliere with ten Branches and gilt socketts with two knots of Ribbons', and fantastically upholstered furniture, showing that Ireland was well able to rival the restoration wonders of Windsor and Knowle.

This renaissance of 1660 ended in the Williamite wars of 1688 to 1690 and again much was destroyed and lost. The Irish economy did not recover for another quarter of a century and very few great houses and public buildings were put up before 1715. The really tragic implications of the disturbed state of Ireland in the seventeenth century were that practically no furnishings of the period survive, and we have to make do with lists of these gaudy articles, from the dusty pages of inventories, probate court transactions and wills. The furnishings of the early eighteenth-century Irish house are again difficult to track down for so much has disappeared and left the country, and contemporary Irish work such as japanning, walnut and gilt show no particular idiosyncratic differences from their English counterparts. French and Dutch artisans came to Dublin in large numbers during this period and there is a certain amount of continental influence on building and design. This, of course, was equally true in England and the Spanish and trifid foot, the *régence* basket of flowers (Fig. 6), the eagle or bird terminals and, above all, the grotesque mask (Fig. 9), became the standard vocabulary of early eighteenth century Irish ornament, the great difference between England and Ireland being that these features were to stay for a good sixty years.

English pattern-books and the ubiquitous William Kent had considerable influence in Ireland and a letter of 1727 from Lord Burlington's man of affairs, Andrew Crotty, to Lord Shannon clearly illustrates both these points: 'I ought to send . . . the two folio Volumnes of cyclopedia, or the Dictionary of Arts and Sciences, now printing at Messrs. Wm. and John Penny [Halfpenny] in Paul's Churchyard . . . meanwhile Mr. Kent has finished his works and I should be glad to know whether I am to freight a Dutch Flyboat, or a South sea Bottom to convey your cargo of them to the Coast of Ireland'. Other pattern-books were used, such as William Jones' *The Gentleman's or Builders' Companion* of 1739. This book was sold in Dublin in the same year and was the obvious source for the Dublin firm of Francis and John Booker's splendid mirror shown in Figure 12. It forms a useful contrast to the elaborate Irish mahogany example in Figure 11, and the flat carving shown here is typical of products of Dublin workshops of this date.

The over-elaborate and grotesque elements of English early Georgian furniture found the right soil in Ireland. The Irish nobility and gentry had a deep-seated taste for excess both in ornament and in eating and drinking. Massive status-symbol mahogany sideboards groaned with the full panoply of ill-assorted festoons, masks and tassels, supporting a wealth of gold and silver plate. Heavy dresses, bottle-stands (Fig. 10), eagle-finialed settees and grinning card-tables (Fig. 9) all lend their feet and arms to support this hospitable atmosphere of licence and hearty benevolence. It is not for nothing that Lord Orrery wrote to a friend from Cork in 1737: 'O Sacred Silence, How I adore Thee! I have pass'd this day admist the confusion of Babel. I have been at a Feast. Paper Mills, Thunder, and a Kings Kitchen are soft Music to the Noises I have heard. Nonsence and Wine have flowed in plenty, gigantic Saddles of Mutton and Brobdingnaggian Rumps of Beef weighed down the Table, Bumpers of Claret and Bowls of White-Wine were perpetually under my Nose, till at last, unable to bear the Torture, I took Advantage of a Health at which We were all oblig'd to rise, and slipped away, leaving a Hat and Sword to be my representatives'.

It would be an oversimplification to say that all the mahogany furniture made in the Irish workshops of the early eighteenth century reflects the last quotation, for much simple furniture, characterised by solid, quiet and sometimes elegant lines in tea-tables and chairs (Fig. 3), survives. Unfortunately, little of this sober furniture has remained in Ireland as its similarity to American examples has long been recognised and most of the best pieces of Irish mahogany furniture of this type are now in the United States, sometimes even masquerading as American. Dark San Domingo and Honduras mahogany were the favoured woods and they were first imported into Ireland in about 1725.

It was at this time that patriots such as Bishop Berkeley were encouraging native manufacture; for instance, in his *Querist* (1736), he asks 'whether, if the arts of Sculpture and Painting were encouraged among us, we might not furnish our own houses in a nobler manner with our own manufactures?'. Charles Smith, in 1750, described Berkeley's collection of paintings in the Episcopal Palace in Cloyne as being a brilliant method of diffusing the polite arts amongst the 'yahoos' of County Cork, continuing to say 'The great usefulness of *Design*, in the manufactures of stuffs, silks, diapers, damasks, tapestry, embroidery, earthenware, sculpture, architecture, cabinet-work, and an infinite number of such arts, is sufficiently evident'.

From the 1730s onwards, painting, stucco-work and furniture-making made great progress and by 1786 there were twenty-eight cabinet-makers, twelve carvers and gilders, three joiners and upholsterers and six harpsichord- and musical-instrument-makers at work in Dublin. Provincial towns had an average of about three in 1788.

By the 1780s, the individual Irish style of elaborately carved and rounded-off low relief decoration was vanishing under the delicate *paterae*, ovals and polite festoons of Adam's neo-classicism (Fig. 8). The hall of Castle Ward (Fig. 4) with its novel plaster trophies was to be replaced by the chill elegance of the circular saloon in Wyatt's Castlecoole (Fig. 5) – though the heavy paw feet of the Dublin-made circular Regency table standing in it hark back to the previous century.

'We begin like princes and we end like beggars'

The turn of the century, with its attendant Union with England, greatly changed the quality of Irish life. Before 1800, two hundred and sixty-nine peers and three hundred Members of Parliament had Dublin houses, but by 1821 there were only thirty-four peers, thirteen baronets and five Members. New people were at the viceregal court and Dublin dropped back into a middle-class torpor. Many of the nobility and gentry retired in disgust to the country and built splendid houses, a magnificent example being Sir Richard Morrison's Ballyfin House; the Victorian water-colour of its Regency drawing-room (Fig. 7) shows an example of this post-Union magnificence. Elsewhere great houses and great demesnes were starting to decay. Maria Edgeworth puts it best in her novel *Ennui* (1809). Having painted Lord Glenthorn's surprised reaction to the magnificence of the Shelburne Hotel, once Kerry House, in St Stephen's Green, before the ill-fated Union, she continues: '"Ah! sir," said an Irish gentleman, who found me in admiration upon the staircase, "this is all very good, very fine, but it is too good and fine to last; come here again in two years, and I'm afraid you will see all this going to rack and ruin. This is too often the case with us in Ireland; we can project, but we can't calculate; we must have everything upon too large a scale. We mistake a grand beginning for a good beginning. We begin like princes, and we end like beggars."'

11

Author's Photo

12

Author's Photo

Fig. 11 ***Mirror** showing the influence of the arabesques of Jean Bérain, Irish, c.1720. Carved mahogany. (Private Collection.)*

Fig. 12 ***Pedimented mirror** after William Jones, by Francis and John Booker, Dublin, c.1750. Gilt pine. (Author's Collection.)*

THE PRINTS OF IRELAND

Desmond Guinness

The Green Studio

Fig. 1 ***'Perspective view of a Bleach Green'*** *designed and engraved by William Hincks, published in London, 1791. Dedicated to 'the Right Honble Lord Visct Kilwarlin and Fairford', this view taken in Co. Down shows 'the methods of Wet and Dry Bleaching, and the outside View of a Bleach Mill on the most approved construction'. The inscription also specifies that the four things seen (other than the courting couple), are: '1. Dry Bleaching; 2. Wet D°; 3. Bleach Mill; and 4. An old Mill.*

Old prints provide valuable information about architecture in Ireland during the eighteenth century, as well as recording contemporary Irish life

Occasionally an artist has the good fortune to find himself in the right place at the right moment, and this was never more true than when James Malton made his series of drawings of Dublin buildings in 1790–91. The views are well known from their publication which began in the following year. They came out in sets of four, and the reproduction in etching and aquatint was done by Malton himself. By the year 1799, the series of twenty-five plates had been published (the view of the Library in Trinity College making the odd number) and they were sold as a bound volume for eight guineas complete with a portfolio or extra cover. 'The entire of the views were taken in 1791 by the author', runs the preface, 'who, being experienced in the drawing of architecture and perspective, has delineated every object with the utmost accuracy . . .'. Malton's 'experience' could not have been acquired at a better place for one who was to produce views of Dublin buildings; for three years he had been employed as a draughtsman in the office of James Gandon, the architect of the Custom House and the Four Courts. In his *Dictionary of Irish Artists*, Strickland writes that 'for breaches of confidence and many irregularities, he was dismissed'.

Fig. 2 '*A Correct Map of Ireland,* *Divided into its Provinces, Counties, and Baronies', dedicated to the Hon. Sir William Robinson by Charles Price, I. Senex and I. Maxwell, London, 1711. Engraving. (Author's Collection.)*

Fig. 3 ***'Perspective View of the Linen Hall in Dublin'****, designed and engraved by William Hincks, published in London, 1791. Dedicated to 'the very Respectable the Linen Merchants and Manufacturers of Ireland, the Conductors of that Great and Beneficial Staple of our Country', this view shows 'the Boxes and Bales of Linen ready for Exportation, the Emblems of their Industry'.*

Fig. 4 ***Custom House, Dublin*** *from James Malton's* Picturesque and Descriptive Views of the City of Dublin *(1792–99).*

Fig. 5 ***View of the Parliament House, College Green, Dublin,*** *by James Malton, Dublin, 1790. Etching and aquatint. Now the Bank of Ireland, the former Parliament House is seen here in an early edition of the print. The pigs being driven past were erased from later editions, as they were felt to detract from the dignity of the House, but the man with his raised stick remained. This print and others in the series of views by Malton mark the high point in Irish engraving. Their accuracy, beauty and clarity was never surpassed.*

2

Figure 5 shows a rare version, dated 1790, of Malton's view of the Parliament House, now the Bank of Ireland. In the left foreground may be seen a man driving two pigs in front of Pearce's noble portico. In deference to the dignity of parliament these were later erased and in the more common version published in 1793 the pigs are no longer there, although the man driving them, with stick raised, may still be seen.

Malton's *Views* contain groups of figures which, quite apart from their decorative nature, add charm and variety to the scene. They are of value to the social historian as a record of daily life, of clothes, uniforms, carriages and so on. But buildings have pride of place; towards the end of the eighteenth century there was unfortunately a general tendency to push these into the background, at least as far as the country house was concerned. The setting became more important than the house and, worse still from the architectural historian's point of view, whole plates would sometimes be taken up with views of wild landscape without a building in sight.

A fine series of views of Irish country houses is

3

The Green Studio

4

R. B. Fleming

5

The Green Studio

the twenty-four plates published by Thomas Milton in sets of four between 1783 and 1793. The twelve that are the most interesting from the architectural standpoint were re-issued in 1963, complete with Milton's descriptions of the houses and the original subscribers' list, by the Irish Georgian Society. Milton's description of Leinster House, designed by the German architect Richard Castle, often known as Castel or Cassels, has the following footnote: 'As the name of *Castel* will frequently occur in the course of this work, some account of that *Architect* will be given in a future number which it is presumed will not be unacceptable'. But the promised treatise never appeared, and Milton seems to have stayed in Ireland only from 1783 to 1786, issuing the last of the *Views of Seats* from London. His engravings were taken from the drawings or paintings of leading artists of the day.

Another proposal that unfortunately came to nothing was put forward in 1753 by George Faulkner, Swift's publisher. He intended to publish a work to be entitled *Vitruvius Hibernicus* containing 'the plans, elevations and sections of the most regular and elegant buildings, both public and private, in the Kingdom of Ireland, with variety of new designs, in large folio plates, engraven on copper by the best hands, and drawn either from the buildings themselves, or the original designs of the architect'. The nearest thing to an Irish *Vitruvius* was the work of Pool and Cash, who published the elevations of the more important Dublin buildings in the year 1780. In some cases they must have had access to the architect's drawings. For example, it is interesting to see Thomas Ivory's intended elevation for the Blue-Coat School, which was subsequently modified for reasons of economy.

The vignettes surrounding maps of towns and counties in Ireland often depict buildings and monuments, and one of the most fascinating of these is Brooking's map of Dublin, published in London in 1728. *The statue of George ye 1st on Essex Bridge* is a curious reminder of the 'popularity' of the Hanoverians in Dublin at that date. The equestrian statue of the King was put on an island in the Liffey, linked to the apex of Essex bridge, its approach guarded by twin sentry-boxes. As if this protection was likely to be insufficient, there was an iron railing round it and spikes protruded at water level in case of approach by water. The statue is no longer there, and Dublin is the only capital city in Europe without an equestrian statue; they have all been blown up.

Noble and Keenan's map of County Kildare, 1752, has a vignette of the Conolly Folly, the remarkable eye-catcher built to 'answer a vistow at the bake of Castletown House' in 1740, a year of great hardship on account of the severe winter in 1739. Also appearing in a vignette on this map is the only engraving to show Carton, formerly the seat of the Dukes of Leinster, with its curved colonnades which were removed in 1817 when the third Duke added to the house. J. Rocque, the French cartographer, produced an engraved map of Dublin in 1756 with incredibly detailed information, including the layout of every garden, and even marking every tree. Kildare House (later Leinster House) is shown in one of the vignettes; it was when this great town palace was sold in 1817 that Carton was altered. Rocque's map of County Dublin came out in 1760, and here the information

6

The Green Studio

7

The Green Studio

8

The Green Studio

Fig. 6 ***'Winding, Warping with a new improved Warping Mill, and Weaving'***, *designed and engraved by William Hincks, published in London, 1791.*
This plate was dedicated to 'the Right Honble the Earl of Hertford, Visct Beauchamp, Lord Conway, Baron of Bagley and Baron of Killaltagh in Ireland and Knight of the Most Noble Order of the Garter'.

Fig. 7 ***Russborough, Co. Wicklow*** *from* Views of Seats *by J. P. Neale, engraved by T. Barber, London, 1826. Built for the 1st Earl Miltown, now the home of Sir Alfred Beit, Russborough was built by Richard Castle in about 1745. This view comes from Neale's massive edition of views, published mainly between 1818 and 1833, which were reasonably accurate.*

Fig. 8 ***The East End and the South Side of the Cathedral Church of Derry*** *from Dheulland's series of Irish cathedrals published by James Ware, 1739–46.*

on park and garden layouts is of the greatest interest. The formal terraces at Powerscourt (which is included in spite of the fact that it is in County Wicklow) are shown to have existed in 1760, giving the lie to the theory that they were created in the Victorian period.

The first known mezzotints executed in Ireland were those of one Thomas Beard in 1729, but as he stayed only for a short time in Dublin his work is scarce. In 1742 John Brooks announced proposals for a series of one hundred mezzotint portraits by subscription, and in the following year he was to have engraved eight country seats of which only two appeared. In 1746 he left Ireland but his assistant, Andrew Miller, carried on in his place. Miller's last dated plate was issued in 1756 and he died in 1763. Strickland lists sixty mezzotints done by him in Dublin, including two of Deàn Swift after paintings by Francis Bindon, engraved in 1743 and 1744. Thomas Frye's curious, haunting mezzotints of heads appeared from 1759 to 1762 and are perhaps the most sought by collectors today.

Jonathan Fisher was a highly competent topographical artist who was born in Ireland and was supervisor of stamps in the Stamp Office from 1778 to 1809. He is best remembered for the views of Killarney based on his own paintings, but, apart from wild landscapes, he skilfully painted many buildings and estates, although his views were somewhat romanticised. William Hincks issued twelve plates based on the linen manufacture in Northern Ireland in 1782 (Figs. 1, 3 and 6).

Some English engravers, when producing sets of views, would include the odd Irish property in order to widen the market for the series. So careless were they that not only was the topography often inaccurate, but sometimes even the county was given wrongly: 'Trim Castle, Co. Antrim', for instance, instead of 'Co. Meath'. There is an engraving of 'Cartown, the Seat of His Grace the Duke of Leinster', which looks something like Chatsworth but absolutely nothing like Carton.

Neale's massive edition entitled *Views of Seats*, mostly English, includes the more important Irish houses and appears to have been reasonably accurate (Fig. 7). It appeared between 1818 and 1833 and has been reproduced for distribution through the print shops in recent years.

Robert Wyse Jackson

Irish Silver

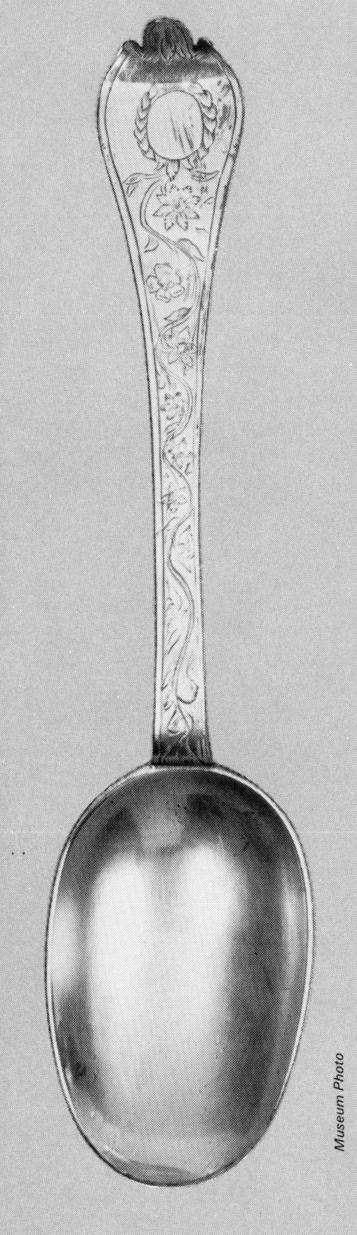

Good workmanship, greater rarity and subtle differences in design from its English counterpart make Irish silver both interesting and valuable to the collector

Brilliant metalwork of three very different kinds has been made in Ireland at three different times in its history. The first was during the early Christian period, when such masterpieces as the eighth-century Ardagh Chalice were created. The craftsmen of this period generally made use of a variety of base and precious metals, an abundance of jewelling and enamelling and an unlimited amount of interlacing of the kind which is seen at its most elaborate in the Book of Kells.

The arrival of the Normans in Ireland in 1170 brought a rapid change of style, and during the following centuries it seems that silver was inspired by the western European gothic tradition. Surviving examples include the De Burgo O'Malley Chalice of 1494 and the 1418 mitre and crosier of Bishop Cornelius O'Dea of Limerick. These are the finest pontificals in the country; they carry the signature of an Irish craftsman, Thomas O'Carryd.

The third and most important period began in 1637, when domestic silver was first made. In so far as it has survived, earlier work seems to have been almost entirely ecclesiastical; now came the beginnings of Irish-made spoons, tankards, drinking-cups, porringers and other such objects. Dublin, the centre of this new activity, was very much a capital city, and had close links with Bristol. It was therefore a city where English as well as Irish craftsmen were working, and who were later to be joined by exiled French Huguenot silversmiths of great skill – men with such names as Francis Girard,

Museum Photo

Fig. 1 ***Spoon** by R. Goble, Cork, 1700. Length* $7\frac{1}{2}$ *ins. (Victoria and Albert Museum, London.)*

Fig. 2 ***Spoon** by Jonathan Buck, Limerick, c.1740. Length* $9\frac{1}{8}$ *ins. (Victoria and Albert Museum.)*

Fig. 3 ***Spoon** by David Pete, Dublin, 1765. Length* $8\frac{1}{4}$ *ins. (Victoria and Albert Museum.)*

Museum Photo

Fig. 4 ***Three dish-rings** by John Lloyd, Dublin, c.1770–80.*
More common in Ireland than elsewhere, the dish-ring was one of the best examples of the mid-eighteenth century rococo style. They have been called 'potato-rings' mistakenly since Victorian times, when they were believed to have been used for serving boiled potatoes. In fact, they were intended to keep bowls of steaming 'bishop' (hot punch) from marking the polished mahogany of a dining-table. They are always pierced, frequently with elaborate patterns, as on these examples. (National Museum of Ireland, Dublin.)

Fig. 5 ***Sauce-boat** by Thomas Walker, Dublin, c.1738.*
This superb piece, though Irish in character, would stand comparison with rococo work from anywhere in Europe. (National Museum of Ireland.)

Fig. 6 ***Monteith** or punch-bowl by Thomas Bolton, Dublin, 1704. Silver-gilt.*
Many Irish designs are virtually indistinguishable from English pieces of the same date. This fine monteith is of a standard design of the late seventeenth and early eighteenth centuries. (National Museum of Ireland.)

Fig. 7 ***Cake-basket** by John Lloyd, Dublin, 1772.*
Irish silver was often more sound, simple and workmanlike than its English counterparts at this date, since the shops made only a fraction of what came from large English metal-working centres such as Birmingham and Sheffield. (National Museum of Ireland.)

Fig. 8 ***Tankard** by Robert Goble, Cork, c.1695.*
The greatest silversmith of Cork, Robert Goble, made the remarkable mace of the Cork Guilds as well as many fine pieces of domestic silver. (National Museum of Ireland.)

John Letablère and Isaac D'Olier.

In December 1637, a royal charter was granted to the Dublin Goldsmiths' Company. This organisation still flourishes and by law it still assays all silver made in Ireland. The Assay Office, Goldsmiths' Hall, which contains original records and some early historical relics, is situated in the precincts of Dublin Castle and is directed by Captain Le Bas, a member of a Huguenot family recorded as working in Dublin in Georgian times.

It is common knowledge that hallmarks were introduced in order to guarantee a standard of purity in gold and silver pieces, and to prevent fraud. (The Dublin Assay Office has a curious collection of fakes, which were seized by law.) London introduced a mark as long ago as the fourteenth century; in Dublin the first marks were used in 1637–38. The marks were put on with individual punches, the number of which increased as the years went by. They began with a mark of origin, a date-letter, and a maker's mark. The mark of origin has always been a crowned harp. The date-letter is an alphabetical code which enables the year of manufacture to be discovered. The maker's mark is a private sign, generally the initials of the individual silversmith.

'This day ye duty came on'

Following the introduction of hallmarks, as a work-book in the archives of the Dublin company puts it under 21 April, 1730, 'This day ye duty came on'. The duty was sixpence an ounce, certified by a stamp of Hibernia, a figure very like Britannia, but holding a harp and a palm-leaf. Very often, when Hibernia was added, the date-letter was left out. This creates difficulties in dating Dublin silver. Some years later, in 1805, the exchequer charged the buyers of silver a further sixpence, and a mark of the Sovereign's head was added. George III looks to the right, George IV to the left, William IV to the right, and Queen Victoria to the left. After 1890, the duty disappeared, as did the Sovereign's head; but Hibernia remained. Ireland never had an equivalent of the English 1697–1720 Britannia Standard of higher silver content.

It may well be asked in what way, apart from markings, Irish silver differs from its English equivalent during the Georgian period. It is known that old Waterford glass was based on English designs, and it is interesting to see whether the same applies to Irish silver and workmanship.

At first sight the similarities are greater than the differences, yet practice enables one to detect the latter. For example, the bright-cutting on Limerick-made spoons is unlike that practised elsewhere. Late eighteenth-century Cork silver is highly distinctive. Dublin silver of the era is sound, simple and workmanlike, which is to be expected from shops which made only a fraction of what came from Birmingham or Sheffield.

Moreover, it is arguable that Ireland produced some eighteenth-century items of silver which can be claimed as more Irish than English. One is a mid-eighteenth-century pierced butter-dish, often made in the Chinese style, and probably originating from Huguenot influence on Irish workshops. The Dublin National Museum has an example which shows a shepherd leering at a maiden from behind an unmistakably Irish Round Tower. This mid-eighteenth-century rococo spirit is seen at its best in the dish-ring, a piece of table-ware far commoner in Ireland than elsewhere (Fig. 4). The word 'dish', in this context, means 'bowl', and in fact this circular stand was intended to keep bowls of steaming 'bishop' (hot punch) from marking the polished mahogany of a dining-table. It is certainly a misnomer to call them 'potato-rings', and the Victorians were incorrect to serve boiled jacket-potatoes in them, wrapped up in a linen table-napkin; it would be proper to balance a bowl of cooked potatoes on one.

A wide variety of small, collectable items

Again, there was a considerable vogue throughout the second half of the eighteenth century for cups with two harp-shaped handles. It would be unwise to say that these were exclusively Irish, but the harp design was much in vogue in the Dublin shops. Further, the helmet-shaped cream-jugs of the first half of the eighteenth century are distinctively Irish.

The variety of small silver pieces was enormous, and there are plenty of collectable items. It is interesting to find an advertisement of 1765 which lists the most popular items stocked by a provincial silversmith and jeweller. This was issued by Collins Brehon, a freeman of Limerick city, who had his establishment opposite the Exchange under the sign of 'The Two Blue Posts'. The advertisement says that 'he makes all kinds of repeating watches and mends them in the best and safest manner . . . the said Brehon has a large assortment of touched plate, Butterboats, large and small ditto, large and small cups, Variety of touched Shoe and Knee Buckles and a large assortment of Jewellery work from the maker in Dublin, such as paste and stone, shoe and knee buckles, Garnet Hoops, Gold set lockets, Rings of different kinds, Pebble rings set around with garnets, watches, &c., he will engage; also plain and chased Coffee pots, and plate-handled knives and forks, with Cases, with several other articles too tedious to mention. N.B. He will give the highest price for old Gold and Silver and for Silver and Gold lace'.

A charm which comes from the personal and the intimate

Brehon's advertisement is a reminder that no account of old Irish silver can be complete without a note about the provincial makers of the Georgian period. Their work has a charm which comes from the personal and the intimate; it was sound and competent hand-made work, and it was up to the standard of English work in the lesser towns. A case in point is that of a mid-seventeenth-century Bandon silversmith called John Moore, who was asked to make a chalice for Cloyne Cathedral. Cloyne was a remote, tiny village, and Bandon a small market town, but John Moore's work was in no way inferior to that of more sophisticated silversmiths. It appears that he borrowed the finely made contemporary London chalice from his parish church as a model. The copy is admirable and completely competent. It has no hallmark, not

4

Museum Photo

5

Museum Photo

6

Museum Photo

7

Museum Photo

8

Museum Photo

having been sent to Dublin. As an alternative, some makers used their full names, for example the seventeenth-century Fennell of Ennis, who signed the Franciscan chalices there.

It is to be expected, Irish conditions being what they were, that few provincial silversmiths sent their wares to Dublin. In small towns no guarantee of quality would be needed; each maker was known far too well to make fraud worth while.

Very little silver was made north of a line drawn between Dublin and Galway. The 'red hand' mark found on a few ancient pieces, once believed to have been made in Belfast, is now said to indicate Maltese silver. South of the line, however, a good many towns had their silversmiths. During the late seventeenth and early eighteenth centuries, a number of town marks existed. Youghal had a yawl; Galway a boat with furled sails on the yard-arm, or an anchor; Cork a tower and a three-masted ship, sometimes combined, sometimes separate. A very few examples exist of a tower indicating Kilkenny; Limerick had a two-towered castle-gate and a five-pointed star, sometimes with wavy beams. As the eighteenth century wore on these local marks died out, and only Cork and Limerick continued to produce identifiable marks. These are confusing, however, since both used the word 'sterling' or its abbreviations. This means that a Limerick piece can only be told from a Cork piece when the initials, or the style, of the maker are known or occasionally by a little fleur-de-lis mark.

Cork silver is still collectable, though rare, and tends to be found in its native county. In the middle of the Cromwellian period, on 21 May, 1656, the goldsmiths of Cork were incorporated as a Guild together with the braziers, pewterers, founders, plumbers, white-plate-workers, glaziers, saddlers and upholsterers of the city. The Guild was known as 'The Society of Goldsmiths of Cork'. The multiplicity of trades gave Robert Goble, Cork's greatest silversmith, his opportunity in the making of the mace of the Cork Guilds. It is a most remarkable piece of work, and is now in the Victoria and Albert Museum, London.

9

Museum Photo

Fig. 9 ***Coffee-pot** by Thomas Bolton, Dublin, 1696. This fine early pot is decorated with the cut-card work introduced into both England and Ireland by the influx of French Huguenot craftsmen late in the century. (National Museum of Ireland.)*

10

Museum Photo

11

Museum Photo

12

Fig. 12 ***Eighteenth-century Irish silver marks.** Top row: Hibernia, the date-letter for 1747 and the crowned harp of Dublin; the yawl of Youghal, c.1712; the anchor of Galway, c.1730. Bottom row: the two-towered castle-gate of Limerick, c.1710; the sterling mark of Limerick and Cork 1700–1800; the tower of Cork, c.1730.*

Fig. 10 ***Pair of sauce-boats** by Robert Calderwood, Dublin,* c.*1737.*
Less elaborately worked than the sauce-boat of a year later illustrated in Figure 5, these pieces were probably intended for more domestic use.
(National Museum of Ireland.)

Fig. 11 ***Jug,** Dublin,* c.*1760.*
Height $6\frac{1}{2}$ ins.
Much Irish silver has charm and a personal quality due to its lack of sophistication.
(Victoria and Albert Museum.)

Fig. 13 ***Three casters** by David King, Dublin, 1699.*
Vertical fluting was popular in Ireland as well as England.
(National Museum of Ireland.)

Cork 'sterling' marked silver from the mid-eighteenth-century is still to be found. One notable partnership was that of Terry and Williams. Carden Terry's work is recorded as early as 1776. In 1795 he went into partnership with his son-in-law, Williams, who died soon afterwards. He continued the partnership with his daughter Jane, and many fine pieces up to 1821 bear the joint initials 'C.T. and J.W.'.

A very satisfactory form of silver collecting in Ireland is provided by spoons. Local pieces are still to be found, very often with local peculiarities such as the pointed handles, the Limerick bright-cutting in the form of the fleur-de-lis, or the Prince of Wales feathers.

Since the output of the Georgian silversmiths in Dublin was minute, and that from Cork and Limerick even less, compared with that from Birmingham, Sheffield or London, it is obvious that Irish pieces have better rarity prospects for the collector. They also show less evidence, on the whole, of mass production.

The peak of Irish output was reached at about the end of the eighteenth century, characterised by the era of bright-cut designs which reflect the light so charmingly. The demand lessened considerably from the time of the potato famine of 1847, since so many formerly well-to-do landlords were beggared and this greatly reduced the number of silversmiths. In Cork the last silversmith of the era seems to have been Kean Mahony who was working around 1840. A modern firm, Egan of Cork, produced some interesting, unassayed locally marked pieces during the Civil War of 1922.

Early Victorian silver, relatively rarer than Georgian, and also cheaper, is well worth collecting. The quality is good, though caution is needed over pieces imported from England and hallmarked in Ireland.

A little later, at the turn of the nineteenth century, came the Celtic revival under Yeats, Synge and Lady Gregory. In Ireland this produced a certain amount of silver with Celtic interlacing, which may well be worth finding.

13

Museum Photo

MUSEUMS AND COLLECTIONS

Irish silver may be seen at the following:

GREAT BRITAIN
London: Victoria and Albert Museum

EIRE
Dublin: National Gallery of Ireland
National Museum of Ireland

FURTHER READING

Hall Marks on Dublin Silver 1730–1772 by Ticher, Delamer and O'Sullivan, Dublin, 1968.
A Guide to Irish Antiques, an annual series published by the Mercier Press, Cork, from 1967.
An Introduction to Irish Silver by the Right Reverend Robert Wyse Jackson, Dublin, 1963.
A Guide to Irish Silver by the Right Reverend Robert Wyse Jackson, publication forthcoming.

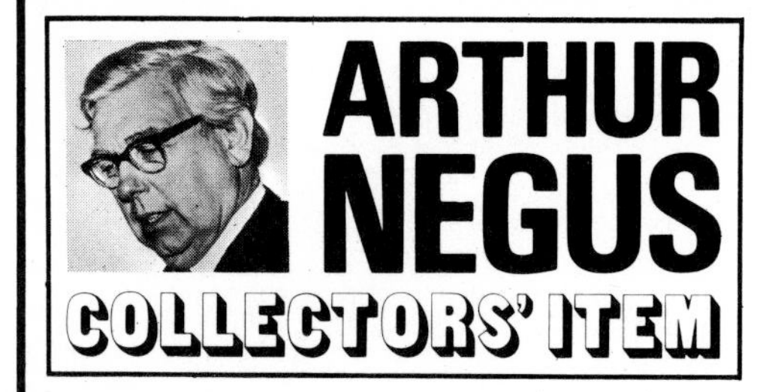

CHEESE-DISHES AND COVERS

The cheese-dish and cover has recently returned to our china shops. But a hundred or more years ago factories all over England were coping furiously with orders for this new and decorative way of presenting cheese on the table, while keeping it fresh.

Cheese-dishes and covers are easily recognisable, usually by their tall, cylindrical, often dome-shaped tops which were made to accommodate even a full-size Stilton.

Shapes and sizes vary considerably, as do glazes and decoration. Agate-glazed dishes by Macintyre are some of the most sought after. There are also earlier pre-Victorian caneware dishes. A well known maker was John Turner of Stoke-on-Trent, whose products became known as Turnerware. There were also the wedge-shaped dishes made to look like a chunk of cheese and variations including cows' heads which demonstrated the connection with the dairy product they covered.

Great factories, too, followed the trend and Wedgwood produced cheese-dishes in his familiar blue Jasper ware. These are rare, much sought and seldom to be had at a bargain price.

William Brownfield, who worked in earthenware and bone china at Cobridge, Staffordshire, also made cheese-dishes and covers. He was most adventurous and experimented with a variety of 'masculine' designs, one of which was his pretty but bold castle pattern decorated with ivy.

There is no greatly representative public collection of cheese-dishes and covers. The Stoke-on-Trent museum has a few examples as does the Victoria and Albert Museum. The textbooks reveal little or nothing. It is really up to the interested collector to do his own research, although this can be difficult as dishes are often unmarked.

Collecting Hints

Many covers on cheese-dishes have, because of their weight, been cracked and repaired. While a repaired example should not be spurned it often pays to look for the perfect specimen. Do however look carefully when making a purchase. If you see an item you want for your collection, buy it; tomorrow someone else may have snapped it up. Some dishes and covers have a date-stamp underneath them; these make an exciting addition to a collection as they tell the month and year of manufacture. Beware of copies.

Prices

A good dish and cover is seldom obtainable for less than £10. This would seem to be a very good buy but another, more interesting, example might cost anything up to £30 and even this price would not be exorbitant for an exceptional piece.

Stall X2, Antiquarius, London S.W.3

Crewe Read & Harrison, London S.W.6

Top: ***Cheese-dish and cover,*** *probably Minton,* c.*1870. £23.*

Above: ***Ivy-clad castle design dish and cover*** *by William Brownfield, Staffordshire. Incised with maker's mark and date mark (indistinct)* c.*1865. £28.*

Opposite: ***Stilton dish and cover*** *with inside glaze. Fine quality dishes of this sort were made* c.*1890. £28.*

Below left: ***German cheese-dish and cover.*** *Marked: 'Mehlem F.A.', Bonn, Rhineland,* c.*1880. £6.50.* Centre: ***Cover and dish*** *by S. Fielding and Co. Stoke. 1890–1900. £5.* Right: ***Cow's head dish and cover,*** c.*1850. Unmarked but almost certainly Staffordshire. £20.*

Bridge Collection and Crewe Read & Harrison, London S.W.6

David & Penny Newlove, Chelsea Antique Market, London S.W.3: R. Todd-White

1

A. C. Cooper

Waterford and Other Irish Glass

Geoffrey Wills

From Waterford in particular, but also Cork, Dublin and Belfast, came the elaborately cut pieces which are synonymous in the public mind with the best in Irish glass

Fig. 1 **Four salts and a caddy,** *c.1785–1800. Blue glass, the caddy mounted with silver, height of salts $2\frac{3}{4}$ ins. (Cecil Davis Ltd., London.)*

Fig. 2 **Water-jug** *marked 'Waterloo Co Cork', 1815–35. Moulded base and engraved ornament, height 6 ins. The Waterloo Glass House Company was founded in the year of the battle of Waterloo, 1815, and went bankrupt after twenty years. (Delomosne and Son, Ltd., London.)*

Fig. 3 **Covered vase on a square foot,** *c.1800. Height 11 ins. This fine vase relies on good proportions with simple mouldings and fluting for effect. (Cecil Davis, Ltd.)*

Fig. 4 **Condiment set,** *c.1825. The holder silver plate, the bottles cut with diamonds in the Irish style, overall height $9\frac{1}{4}$ ins. The diamond patterns were cut by hand on an iron wheel and polished on a wooden wheel. (City Museum and Art Gallery, Plymouth.)*

The successful manufacture of glass in Ireland in the last quarter of the eighteenth century and the first half of the nineteenth was due entirely to political causes. The more important of these stimulated the expansion of industries in the country, many of which had remained in a state of stagnation struggling to endure against great odds.

Irish manufacturers in general had received little or no encouragement during the eighteenth century, when they were prohibited from exporting their goods and sales were limited to the home market. This condition was imposed by the English government in deference to the wishes of their own manufacturers, who were content to have a steady, if small, number of buyers conveniently close at hand. However, the outbreak of the American War of Independence in 1775 led to a threat that the French might invade Ireland in order to launch an attack on England. The possibility of such an event gave the Irish an opportunity that they did not hesitate to exploit. Under the able leadership of the statesman and orator Henry Grattan, they were able to procure constitutional freedom from Westminster, and no longer did the Dublin parliament have meekly to await London approval before their decisions became law. Grattan also obtained for the Irish the right to trade wherever they wished, and thenceforward they were permitted to make what they pleased and sell to whomsoever would buy.

The English glass-makers had to pay a duty on their products which lessened their sales by making the wares expensive; its imposition also caused inconvenience. Customs agents were stationed in every glasshouse, where they checked all the processes and ensured that the full and exact amount of duty was paid. With a corps of tax-collectors conveniently stationed wherever they were required, it was not a difficult matter merely to increase the duty whenever more money was required. This was done in 1777; four years later the process was repeated and the makers began to look about them for ways of circumventing the hardship.

Ireland now offered an opportunity to glass-makers, for in that country glass was free of tax and there were no restrictions on trade. Soon after 1780 Englishmen began to cross the Irish Sea to escape the extortions of their government and endeavour to increase their profits. At the same time, the Irish themselves were not slow to take advantage of the chance for which they had waited so long.

One firm of glass-makers had managed to prosper in Dublin with the aid of financial assistance from the Royal Dublin Society, which had been founded to encourage local arts and manufactures. Richard Williams and Company was founded in about 1764 by a group of Welshmen, and nine years later was able to announce that they 'had brought the manufacture to as great perfection as carried on abroad'. In 1777 they built a new glass-house in Marlborough Street, Dublin, and continued in business until 1829.

The Waterford Glass-House was established in 1783

It is, however, the glasshouses that were established from 1783 onwards, by or in conjunction with English craftsmen, that resulted in the production of the distinctive Irish glass. The best-known and longest lasting of these was the one which advertised in the *Dublin Evening Post* on 4 October 1783: 'Waterford Glass-House. George and William Penrose having established an extensive Glass Manufactory in this city, their Friends and the Public may be supplied with all kinds of plain and

Raymond Fortt

3

Wallace Heaton Ltd.

4

Robert Chapman

cut Flint Glass, useful and ornamental; they hope when the Public know the low Terms they will be supplied at, and consider the vast expence attending this weighty undertaking, they will not take offence at their selling for Ready Money only. They are now ready to receive orders, and intend opening their Warehouse the 1st of next month. Wholesale Dealers and Exporters will meet with proper Encouragement. Sept. 22, 1783'.

The two Penroses were brothers, moneyed merchants with no knowledge of the processes of glass-making but sufficient business acumen to seize the opportunity of the moment. The essential expertise was provided by an Englishman, John Hill, who had been working at Stourbridge and left there for Waterford in company with what was described as 'the best set of workmen that he could get in the county of Worcester'. Hill stayed only three years and left suddenly for an unknown reason, but not before he had passed on all his secrets to a fellow-Englishman, Jonathan Gatchell. As a result, Gatchell was elevated from clerk to manager and in time succeeded to ownership of the firm. Relatives carried on after him until 1851, when the business was closed, leaving behind it a reputation that remains undiminished today.

Less than one hundred miles to the south-west of Waterford is the city of Cork, where no fewer than three glasshouses were opened and closed in a period of sixty years. The first of these was the Cork Glass Company which was established in 1783, the same year as that at Waterford. It remained in business until 1818, but three years before that, in the year of the battle of Waterloo, a competitor appeared on the scene, appropriately named the Waterloo Glass House Company. Finally, in 1818 came the Terrace Glass Works, which was closed in 1841, six years after the Waterloo Company had gone bankrupt.

Fig. 5 **Decanter,** *one of a pair marked 'Cork Glass Co', c.1800. The bodies part-moulded with flutes and cut with shallow patterns, height 9¾ ins. The Cork Glass Company was established in 1783, the same year as Waterford, and remained in business until 1818. (Delomosne and Son, Ltd.)*

5

Raymond Fortt

Many small makers came and went

Other manufactories in the country were at Dublin and Belfast. In the capital, Dublin, in addition to the Williams glassworks mentioned above, was that of Charles Mulvaney which started in about 1785, but although he called himself a maker it is possible that he dealt in goods made by others. Soon afterwards Thomas and John Chebsey were operating a glasshouse near Ballyborough Bridge, but it closed after only ten or eleven years in 1797 or 1798. Belfast, in the north of the country, was the site of a works established by a Bristol man, Benjamin Edwards. He was succeeded by his son of the same name who ran the concern from 1812 until about 1829, and successive members of the family kept it running until about 1870.

The foregoing were the makers who came and went, but while they can be identified by name their products are mostly indistinguishable and cannot always be differentiated from contemporary English productions. Being free of tax, the Irish could be more lavish with their material but, in spite of the level of duty payable in England, equally heavy pieces were made there. It was the imposition of a tax in Ireland in 1825 that slowly but surely killed off what had been a short-lived industrial and artistic venture with considerable potential for the future.

In the pioneer English book on glass, *Old English Glasses*, published in 1897, the author Albert Hartshorne wrote 'There is no information that the glass made at Dublin and Cork had any special characteristics of metal or form, beyond those common to the generality of glasses in England at the end of the eighteenth century; but Waterford glass is usually to be distinguished by its pale blue tinge'. The possibility of Waterford products being easily recognisable in comparison with other varieties was seized on by the uninformed and only in recent years has the view been modified. A dealer who specialised in Irish glass wrote in the twenties that it differed from English because it is 'tougher and stronger than any other', 'gives a sense of warmth to the touch', and while 'British glass has a clear, definite, bright ring' much of Irish make has what was termed a 'peculiar throb'. Doubtless it was good sales-talk, but it does not withstand examination. The blue and grey tinge found in a proportion of surviving old glass, which may or may not be Irish, is due only to faults in manufacture such as inaccurate weighing and careless mixing of ingredients.

Waterford is stated to have made a point of attempting to produce a perfectly colourless glass, and as long ago as 1920 Dudley Westropp, then Curator of the Irish National Musuem, Dublin, wrote quite firmly: 'As far as I can judge from examining many authentic pieces, the metal of Waterford glass is much whiter than that of other of the old Irish glasshouses'.

Marked by slightly raised wording under the base

A few of the Irish manufacturers marked their products, and provided future collectors with indisputable evidence of some portion of their output. In each instance the marking takes the form of slightly raised wording under the base of the article, which was executed during its making by blowing the object in a mould prepared with the necessary lettering. Carelessness in the glassworks and subsequent wear and tear often result in the marks being difficult to decipher and sometimes they are so faint as to be overlooked altogether. The makers concerned and their marks are: B. EDWARDS BELFAST; CORK GLASS CO.; PENROSE WATERFORD; WATERLOO CO., CORK.

In addition there were a number of retailers who had goods marked in a similar manner with their names: ARMSTRONG ORMOND QUAY; J. D. AYCKBOWN DUBLIN or J D A; MARY CARTER & SON 80 GRAFTON ST., DUBLIN; FRANCIS COLLINS DUBLIN; C M & CO. (Charles Mulvaney).

Inscriptions, crests and Masonic symbols are now rarely found

The majority of marked pieces are wine-decanters and finger-bowls, while water-jugs and dishes have been recorded in small numbers. The decanters, bowls and jugs share the feature of a row of short, upright shallow flutes round the lower part of the body. These were moulded and show none of the sharp precision of cutting. The decanters of the various makers exhibit variations, but they are less pronounced than was once thought and

6

7

Fig. 6 ***Pair of boat-shaped salts,*** c.1800. *Diamond cut, height $3\frac{3}{8}$ ins.*
Elaborately cut table wares are generally considered to be characteristic of Irish glass.
(Delomosne and Son, Ltd.)

Fig. 7 ***Square-based turnover bowl,*** c.1800. *Height 8 ins.*
Most esteemed of all Irish glass wares are the massive serving bowls, such as this 'turnover' bowl named for its curled rim; they glisten with reflected light from their cut surfaces.
(Delomosne and Son, Ltd.)

it is unsafe to rely on them for identification in the case of an unmarked example.

Some of the decanters and other articles were devoid of ornament except for the fluting, but many were given cut or engraved decoration. Cork noticeably favoured use of the vesica, a pointed oval, which frequently appears on pieces from the city, but occasionally more ambitious patterns were attempted there and elsewhere. Inscriptions, crests and Masonic symbols are recorded, and while probably plentiful at one time they are now rare.

Although the decanters and other marked pieces are unquestionably Irish in origin, they are not in the public mind characteristic of that country's glass. Truly representative are the elaborately cut pieces for use at the dining-table; pieces that recall the name 'Waterford' throughout the world. Examples range from covered vases and jars for holding all kinds of foodstuffs, drinking-glasses, cream-jugs, salts, and bottles for oil, vinegar and flavourings. Of them all, the most esteemed are the massive serving-bowls, some with curled rims ('turnover' bowls), which glisten with hundreds of points of light reflecting from their cut surfaces. The cutting was performed by holding the blank article against revolving wheels of various materials, deep cuts being made with a wheel of iron fed with a trickle of water and sand which did the work. When the incisions had been made they were polished on wooden wheels using a soft powder. Before starting, the pattern was marked out to guide the craftsman, but the completed decoration relied greatly on the experience of his eyes and hands and its charm lies in the human

8

Raymond Fortt

9

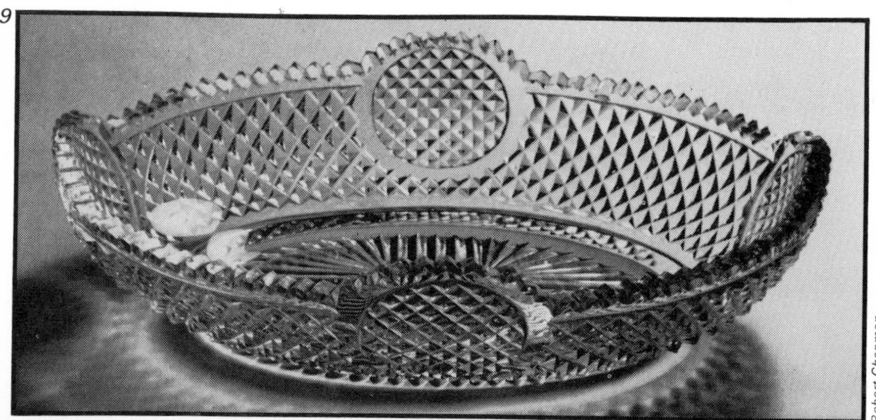

Robert Chapman

10

R. Todd-White

Fig. 8 ***Boat-shaped bowl,*** *c.1790. Flat-cut with a shaped rim, on a moulded foot, height 8 ins.*
Until about 1800, Irish glass often featured shallow 'slices', cut away from the surface or giving a bevel to the rim.
(Delomosne and Son, Ltd.)

Fig. 9 ***Oval bowl,*** *c.1820. Cut with small diamonds on the sides and with radiating flutes beneath the base, width 9 ins.*
At around this date, the 'Age of Exuberance' set into Irish glass-making, and the cutters gave full play to their fancy, using every combination of strokes possible.
(Private Collection.)

Fig. 10 ***Pair of covered sugar-bowls,*** *Irish, c.1790. Cut with a Van Dyck border, height 7 ins.*
One of the charms of Irish glass is that, being cut by hand, it is not always perfectly regular.
(Delomosne and Son, Ltd.)

touch, the slight inaccuracies revealed on close inspection.

The patterns which were in use up to about 1800 were often composed of shallow 'slices' cut away from the surface or giving a bevel to the rim. After that date, the 'Age of Exuberance' set in, and the cutter gave full play to his fancy by using a wide combination of strokes to increase the brilliant effect of his work. Complexity extended to construction, with some of the largest bowls being made with a separate foot, and flat dishes given a base on which to revolve as a 'lazy Susan'. At the 1851 Great Exhibition the Waterford company exhibited a table centrepiece composed of no less than forty pieces, 'so fitted to each other as to require no connecting sockets of any other material'. The Exhibition closed on 11 October, but, alas, the glass-makers had found themselves unable to surmount their business difficulties and had advertised a sale of their entire stock in the September. It was the end of an enterprise that had endured for almost seventy years, but one that remains internationally known today.

In spite of words to the contrary about the alleged colour of Waterford glass, the blue-grey legend persisted for many years. Foreign manufacturers busy supplying the antiques market in the decade 1920 to 1930, carefully tinted their 'genuine Waterford', but took less trouble to make it in correct shapes and with proper cut ornament. It should be added that a new company was started at Waterford in 1948 and makes copies of some of the products of its forerunner. Furthermore, marked decanters have been reproduced, and any with particularly clear wording on them should be examined with extra care.

MUSEUMS AND COLLECTIONS

Irish glass may be seen at the following:

London:	Victoria and Albert Museum
Belfast:	Ulster Museum
Dublin:	National Museum of Ireland

FURTHER READING

Irish Glass: the Age of Exuberance by Phelps Warren, London, 1970.

English and Irish Glass by Geoffrey Wills, London, 1968.

A History of English and Irish Glass (2 vols.) by W. A. Thorpe, London, 1929.

English and Irish Glass by W. A. Thorpe, London, 1927.

Irish Glass by M. S. Dudley Westropp, London, 1920.

THE SPLENDOVR OF THE HIGH RENAISSANCE

Cosimo the Elder (1389–1464)
Lorenzo the Magnificent (1449–92)
Giuliano de' Medici (1453–78)
Cosimo I de' Medici (1519–74)

The arts during the Renaissance flourished in an atmosphere of creative energy which inspired unparalleled sophistication and splendour.

William Gaunt

The High Renaissance in Italy can be viewed as the central phase of the great movement that came after the Middle Ages and as a period of mature splendour following the brilliant developments of the fifteenth century. It was a phase that reached its height in the first half of the sixteenth century, the Italian *cinquecento*, merging later with Mannerism and the beginnings of the Baroque. To the biographer-historian, Giorgio Vasari (1511–74), the first edition of whose *Lives of the Most Eminent Painters, Sculptors and Architects* was published in 1550, it was a time dominated by the mighty Michelangelo whose work was a final perfection, the happy outcome of a long-continuing process of improvement.

Art had grown out of childhood into lusty youth

Vasari saw the 'rebirth' of art and learning in metaphorical likeness to human life. First came childhood, the age of Cimabue and Giotto. The alien influences of 'bad Greek' art – as he called Byzantine art – and northern Gothic were exorcised by a simple purity in which the naturalism of antiquity began to revive. By the fifteenth century, Vasari remarked, art had grown out of the childhood stage and arrived at a lusty youth.

The Renaissance as we now see it was well under way in the city-states of central and northern Italy. Economically prosperous, with a strongly developed civic pride and governed by liberal patrons of the arts, Florence was the supreme example. A city of great wealth, the centre of a financial system that stretched across Europe, vigorous in intellectual life and unrivalled in the production of beautiful things, its scholars, artists and craftsmen were stimulated by the unique liberality in patronage of the Medici family. Cosimo de' Medici (1389–1464) and his grandson, Lorenzo de' Medici (1449–92), expended a considerable part of their enormous fortune acquired by financial operations on the arts. Their Platonic academy was a centre of the humanist culture of the Renaissance where Christian principles existed in harmony with classical philosophy. Scholars were able to study the priceless manuscripts which formed the splendid nucleus of the Laurentian Library, eventually housed in the building designed by Michelangelo, and sculptors and painters derived inspiration from the collection of classical carvings and bronzes in the Medici gardens.

Whether or not one accepts in its entirety Vasari's theory of progress – and modern thinking is dubious of the idea of continued improvement, particularly in the arts – there were changes in the later years of the fifteenth century that signalised fresh developments. Richly illuminated manuscript books, like that which Pope Leo X studies in Raphael's portrait, were still produced, but the introduction of printing gave a new incentive to scholarship. Printing-presses were set up at Rome in 1467, Venice in 1469 and Florence in 1471. The texts of classical authors in printed form required high standards of learning in commentary, translation and the amendment of faulty manuscripts. The spirit of careful research extended to the study of ancient architecture. Even in medieval times the classical tradition had not become extinct in Italy despite the inroads of the gothic movement; the rounded arches and pilasters of the baptistry at Florence (*c.*1290) testify to this. Yet the classical element in architecture was spontaneous and informal until, in the later years of the fifteenth century, principles, methods and proportions were reviewed.

De Architectura, the rediscovered manuscript of the Roman architect Vitruvius, who was an official in the reign of the Emperor Augustus, had a great

2

Scala

Fig. 1 *(frontispiece)* ***Ceiling medallion*** *by Giorgio Vasari (1511–74), mid-sixteenth century. Vasari, painter, architect and author, was responsible for much of the decoration of the Palazzo Vecchio. This medallion shows an episode from Homer's* Odyssey, *in which Penelope, wife of Odysseus, weaves by day the tapestry she unpicks by night. She knows that when it is completed she must marry one of her suitors. (Palazzo Vecchio, Florence.)*

influence in disseminating knowledge of Greek and, more particularly, Roman building methods. This influence was reinforced by the publication in 1485 of *De Re Aedificatoria* by Leon Battista Alberti (1404–72), who was one of the pioneers of revival. Based on the Vitruvian precepts, his work set out mathematical rules for planning and design, including the ideal proportions of the Four Orders: Tuscan, Doric, Ionic and Corinthian. Architectural book-learning of this kind was supplemented by practical demonstration and the measuring of actual ruins of ancient buildings. The result was a stately and dignified style in which mathematical proportions played a large part and the column and pilaster, in varying combinations, were the principal means of decoration.

Full scope for floral, human and grotesque motifs

Each new discovery of classical remains stimulated the arts afresh. Just as the discovery of Pompeii and Herculaneum in the eighteenth century was to bring a neo-classic style into existence, so the discovery in 1488 of the well-preserved stucco decoration of piers and vaults in the substructure of the Baths of Titus and the Golden House of Nero on the Esquiline Hill in Rome began a new era in decoration. The symmetrical type of pattern with its varied systems of curvature and combinations of floral, animal, human and grotesque motifs gave full scope to the ingenuity of artists and was included in the repertoire of design early in the sixteenth century, adaptable to many uses besides mural decoration: to furniture, textiles, metalwork, pottery and jewellery. Raphael and his assistants exploited the style with brilliant virtuosity in the painted stucco ornament of the Loggie of the Vatican. Giulio Romano and Giovanni da Udine produced memorable decorative work, in the style Raphael had revived and adapted, at the Villa Madama, Rome, and the Palazzo del Tè, Mantua. (Fig. 7.)

The palaces of the High Renaissance, in Florence, Genoa, Venice, Verona and elsewhere, testify to the wide distribution of wealth in the Italian cities. Although painting is considered its supreme achievement the sixteenth century in Italy is remarkable also for the galaxy of architects who designed these magnificent buildings, It was Rome, however, that now offered the greatest scope in this field. A succession of ambitious and energetic popes sought to retrieve the neglected and ruinous condition into which the city had fallen during the seventy years of the Papacy's 'Babylonish Captivity' at Avignon. It was intolerable to them that Rome should fail to surpass Florence and Venice in magnificence. Their political ambitions went farther – to bring the city-states under papal rule.

Re-established in prosperity, the papal Court attracted many families of importance to Rome, adding their palaces and villas to the wave of new building. The grandeur of the town palace retained something of the fortress-like simplicity of the Palazzo Riccardi, Florence, designed by Michelozzo.

A place of retreat from the heat of the city

The rural villa was in complete contrast to this formality. It was a place of retreat from the season of excessive heat in the city, designed to accord with nature rather than to conform to Vitruvian rule. Here the wealthy diverted themselves with hunting, card-playing, the composition and recitation of lyric poetry and those musical performances of which the painters give record (Fig. 5). The wealthy dignitaries of the Church and the patrician families who settled in Rome followed in the footsteps of the ancient Romans and built summer resorts in the Alban mountains, among the wooded slopes and waterfalls of Tivoli, Frascati or Castel Gandolfo. Florentines had their villas among the pine-wooded hills of Tuscany; Venetians were able to enjoy liberty of space on the mainland; Genoa offered delightful sites and Como and the north Italian lakes were other favoured localities.

Fig. 2 ***The Villa Maser*** *by Andrea Palladio (1518–80). Palladio, one of the greatest and most influential Italian architects, designed villas in the Veneto to recapture the beauty and perfection of antiquity. At the Villa Maser, built in the 1560s, he treated the whole central block as a temple front, which he wrongly believed to be the format for ancient Roman villas.*

3

Scala

Fig. 3 ***Camera degli Sposi*** *showing paintings by Andrea Mantegna (c.1431–1506), completed in 1474. The Camera degli Sposi has one of the most influential secular decorative schemes of the fifteenth century. It is the earliest instance of illusionistic decoration carried out consistently over walls and ceilings alike and it is, therefore, the natural precursor of the magnificent* trompe l'œil *paintings of the following century. Here the spectator believes he is in an open loggia, where various episodes from the life of the Gonzaga family are taking place. The figures and animals are painted to look as if they could step out of the picture into real space and the figures emerging from behind the pillars and standing in front of them add to the feeling of depth. (Palazzo Ducale, Mantua.)*

Fig. 4 ***Portrait of Eleanora of Toledo*** *by Agnolo Bronzino (1502–72), c.1545. Oil on panel, 45 x 37½ ins.*
Bronzino was court painter to Cosimo I de' Medici (1519–74), first grand duke of Tuscany. This portrait of his wife and son displays with frigid accuracy the details of their faces and costumes and it is typical of the elegant exaggeration affected by the Mannerists.
(Uffizi, Florence.)

Fig. 5 *Detail of musicians from* ***The Marriage at Cana*** *by Paolo Veronese (c.1525–88), 1562–3. Oil on canvas, 262 x 392 ins.*
Although Veronese is ostensibly depicting a biblical scene, he based his painting on a scene that might have taken place at the villa of one of his rich patrons.
(Louvre, Paris.)

Fig. 6 ***Lorenzo de' Medici*** *by Michelangelo (1475–1564), c.1520.*
Michelangelo was trained in his sculpture school and it is fitting that he should have designed the funerary chapel in which Lorenzo and his brother were buried.
(Medici Chapel, San Lorenzo, Florence.)

Villa architecture cast off all restraint. Its designers gave free rein to fancy and indulged in playful exaggeration of classical features of style. The gardens were provided with variety for the eye in the form of belvederes, loggie, grottoes and balustrades. Free-standing, life-size statues of classical gods and goddesses, nymphs and fauns were scattered in profusion about the gardens. The fountain basins of varied and graceful design had their complement of Neptunes, tritons and dolphins.

The Villa Lante, Bagnaia, near Viterbo is a beautiful example of garden design by the architect Giacomo Barozzi da Vignola (1507–73). He was the inventor of the single-vase baluster that appears in the design of the central fountain and again in the court of the monumental Villa Farnese (1547) at Caprarola, near Rome. Vignola also helped to re-introduce and popularise the ancient type of terminal figure, or herm. In Greece, wooden posts topped by the carved head of Hermes had done duty as boundary-posts and milestones. The Romans of Imperial times copied the idea and decorated the gardens of their villas with half-figures growing out of, or sheathed in, stone columns. The renaissance architect was acting in accord with classical precedent in using them to decorate the Caprarola gardens and to ornament the fountain court of the Villa of Pope Julius III at Rome. Andrea Palladio (1518–80) designed villas as harmoniously in accord with nature as the superbly proportioned Villa Malcontenta overlooking the Brenta Canal and as sumptuous as that for the Barbaro family at Maser (Fig. 2), where there are sixty-six rooms and *trompe l'œil* paintings by Veronese.

Furniture grew more elaborate and richer in decoration. The *cassone*, the traditional marriage chest, always an object on which decoration was lavished, grew heavier and was elaborately carved rather than painted like the earlier examples. Rich decoration was applied to tables and the armchairs that now came into use, cabinets, writing-desks, the posts and head- and foot-boards of four-poster beds, Florentine picture frames and the mirrors that were a speciality of Venice.

The craftsman in metal showed a like virtuosity.

7

Fig. 7 ***The Palazzo del Tè Mantua*** *by Giulio Romano (c.1492–1546), 1526–31. Built for Federigo Gonzaga's honeymoon, the Palazzo del Te was also intended as the Duke's summer villa. The plan is largely based on ancient Roman architecture, but Romano has added his own personal note. The details are distorted and used in a completely unclassical way for dramatic effect, while the design of the garden and house are interrelated in an unprecedented manner.*

Sculptors in bronze at Florence, Venice, Padua and Mantua were as ready to apply their skill to finely-wrought candlesticks, door-knockers and fire-dogs as to works of purely aesthetic import. The outstanding example of sculptor-goldsmith, Benvenuto Cellini (1500–1571), produced such diverse masterpieces of the High Renaissance as the statue of Perseus with the head of Medusa in the Loggia dei Lanzi, Florence, and the wonderfully ornate salt-cellar of solid gold made for François I, king of France. The armourers of Milan covered the breastplates, helmets and greaves of suits of armour designed for martial pageantry and pastime rather than war with typical renaissance ornament.

Set against a background of simmering revolt and power-politics

In keeping with all this decorative splendour was the richness of attire, the velvets, silks and gold brocades illustrated in Titian's *La Bella* or Bronzino's *Portrait of Eleonora of Toledo* (Fig. 4); the wife of Cosimo I de' Medici, she is portrayed in a sumptuous patterned dress, overhung with pearls.

Yet the magnificent evolution of the arts was set against an uneasy background of simmering revolt and power-politics. The history of the Medici family includes banishment and assassination. The intellectual freedom of the humanist had its stern complement in the puritanical criticism of men and manners. In Florence Girolamo Savonarola denounced the 'corruption' of the city which for him included the painting of pagan subjects. Neither the Borgia pope, Alexander VI, nor the Florentines could long endure his fiery preaching and he was found guilty of heresy, hanged, and his body ceremoniously burned in public in 1498. A greater revolt was begun when, in 1517, Luther nailed to the church door at Wittenberg his protest against the sale of indulgences, a source of income much favoured by Pope Leo X. But looming large at that moment was a different cause for concern; France, the Empire of Charles V and the Papacy, each conspired to extend its possessions in Italy. The moves and countermoves resulted in the Sack of Rome in 1527 by Charles V's mercenaries and the surrender of Florence to the imperial forces in 1530.

The end of the High Renaissance has been sometimes held to date from these destructive incursions but the pattern of patronage and constructive effort was not broken, however. Pope Clement VII emerged from his six months confinement in the Castel Sant' Angelo with no diminution of interest in art. Michelangelo, after completing the Medici Chapel in San Lorenzo, Florence, with its superb sculptured figures, was commissioned by the Pope in 1534 to paint the altar wall of the Sistine Chapel, the result being his amazing masterpiece, *The Last Judgement*.

There was, however, a change of mood characterised in the arts by the exaggeration of the high renaissance style and a revolt against classical order – a movement now described as Mannerism. Michelangelo himself might be called a herald of Mannerism from the agitated composition of *The Last Judgement* and the restless detail in the buildings he designed. The villas of this time, mannerist in a more light-hearted fashion, had an exaggeration of form that Rome was to turn to propagandist account in the Baroque, the effort to reassert the authority of the Church in outward display against the forces of the Reformation. Distinct as the Baroque style became, it was also the final stage of the Renaissance.

ITALIAN RENAISSANCE VILLAS

The following Italian villas are open to the public:
Villa Lante, near Viterbo.
Palazzo del Tè, Mantua.
Villa Rotunda, near Vicenza.
Also villas at Tivoli, Frascati and Castel Gandolfo near Rome.
The Villa Malcontenta near Vicenza may be visited by permission of the local tourist office.

FURNITURE PALAZZO

1

Museum Photo

2

David van Dijk

3

Pucciarelli

Figs. 1 and 2 ***Cassone or marriage chest,*** Venetian, *c.1500. The ivory inlay of this* cassone *has both Eastern and medieval characteristics typical of northern Italy. (Rijksmuseum, Amsterdam.)*

Fig. 3 ***Armadio, or cupboard,*** *possibly from Mantua, c.1580. The* armadio *developed from the* cassone*; this piece, with its elaborate grotesques, shows the decorative exaggerations of the mannerist style. (Palazzo Davanzati, Florence.)*

Furniture in Italy gradually conformed to the renaissance ideal and expansive public display was replaced by expensive private delight.

Wealthy Italian families in the early years of the fifteenth century took little interest in the furnishing of their palaces. It might appear surprising that those who patronised painters, sculptors, goldsmiths and architects so avidly should consider furniture a necessary but unimportant feature in a room, impermanent and apt to detract from the overall decorative scheme for which, perhaps, one of the greatest fresco painters of the day had been responsible.

In 1400 taste throughout Europe was for carved oak wall-panelling and for panelling on articles of furniture such as the chest; the medieval way of life, and thus the decorative standards, were generally haphazard. A room might contain splendidly ornate silk wall-hangings, rough linen-fold oak panelling, a central fire brazier and an enormous dining-table, all beneath a colourfully painted beamed ceiling. Gradually, however, attitudes towards furniture in Italy were changing; after about 1450 the new design and decorative elements in the Fine Arts were regularly applied to the construction of furni-

FOR THE

Jeremy Cooper

4

Fig. 4 **Cassone**, *North Italian, early sixteenth century. This carved* cassone *illustrates the antiquarian interests of the renaissance artists. The battle scene is derived directly from sarcophagi (stone coffins), while the grotesques on the lid likewise show classical influence. (Ganet Collection.)*

ture – the forms of all furniture conformed to the laws of just proportion, geometric panelling and inlay appeared on the *cassoni*, or marriage chests, and four-poster beds grew classical columns. By the 1530s, the period of mannerist decorative elegance and excesses, furniture had established its position in the decorative whole as the emphasis changed from expansive public display to expensive private delight.

Chests filled with the dowry and belongings of the bride

The principal article of furniture in the Renaissance was the *cassone*, so named because during the marriage procession these large rectangular chests, filled with the dowry and belongings of the bride, were carried through the streets to the groom's palace (Figs. 1, 2, 4 and 8). As they were displayed publicly, these objects were often very expensively and beautifully decorated, sometimes with painted panels executed by the best-known painters of the time; Botticelli and Perugino, for example, are recorded as having executed *cassone* panels. As the cupboard and the chest of drawers only evolved at the beginning of the sixteenth century, the *cassone* was in universal use for the storage of linen, clothes, valuables and all sorts of domestic paraphernalia; there could be as many as fifty *cassoni* in one Florentine palace, placed against the walls as well as in the traditional position at the end of the bed. At first sight the fifteenth century *cassone* may not appear to differ radically from its immediate predecessor, the medieval chest; both objects are basically the same long-box shape, sometimes on feet, otherwise on a flat base, the interior being undivided except for one end where there was frequently a small box-drawer for holding jewels and other valuables. On closer inspection it will be seen that the new formal and decorative characteristics of the *cassone* reflect some of the many and significant stylistic changes of the Renaissance.

The first and most important difference between the medieval chest and the Renaissance *cassone* is one of proportion; the gothic style is in general characterised by spiky elongation of forms, and the medieval chest, of tall, slim proportions, often has carved gothic tracery decorating the front. In fifteenth-century Italy, however, the chest assumed the balanced proportions ordained by classical design and also became a superbly architectural object with applied pilasters, carved friezes and imposingly articulated lids and bases. (Fig. 4.) Many different decorative methods were used; sometimes scenes and figures derived from the Roman running frieze were described in *pastiglia* (moulded and painted plasterwork), as a variation on the painted wooden panel already mentioned.

Naturalistic and geometric use of inlay to give illusions of space

One of the most significant innovations was in the use of illusionistic inlay of wood. The front of the *cassone* was divided evenly by heavily framed square panels in which a naturalistic or geometric pattern was inlaid to give the illusion of space. In the borders there are sometimes geometric abstract patterns derived from illusionistic Roman mosaics under excavation at the time. These devices had a long life as decorative features of European furniture; the rectangular panel in high relief became the principal motif on baroque cabinets, and it was still popular at the end of the eighteenth century. Classical running patterns in various forms have been in continuous use on furniture until the introduction of modern machine methods.

The *cassone* always remains a fascinating, fundamental object in the history of European furniture; not only does it display the first use in furniture of certain important ornamental methods, but from its basic form grew many of the pieces of furniture that were soon to be so familiar. An obvious mutation occurs from the *cassone* into the *cassapanca*, the solidly proportioned wooden-backed bench from which in turn the standard upholstered sofa was eventually to emerge in the seventeenth century. By the beginning of the sixteenth century the *cassone* itself had become more elegant, with concave curved end-sections on tallish feet. It created the basic shape of the commode, although drawers did not yet appear in the front.

The *cassone*, due to its prestige function as a marriage chest, was the only object in which any artistic interest was regularly expressed. Nevertheless, there are other pieces of furniture which have undeniable attractions to our eyes, one of these being the folding X-shaped arm-chair, called either a Savonarola or Dante chair according to certain small differences of form. (Fig. 7.) Although basically pre-renaissance in design, the Savonarola chair has an assured elegance and a sophisticated balance of semi-circular volumes. All chairs had to be easily movable and it is admirable that a collapsible chair should possess such quality of design.

5

Museum Photo

Fig. 5 **Sgabello, or stool,** *one of a pair, Florentine, c.1500. Walnut decorated with gilding. Despite its small size, this stool has a marvellously architectural appearance, both in its proportions and in the use of a frieze motif. The carved scroll-work displays a roundness of treatment that differs from mannerist use of the same forms. (Victoria and Albert Museum, London.)*

The lady of the house was surrounded by rugs and cushions from the East

Towards the end of the century a completely new type of chair emerged called the *sgabello*. (Fig. 5.) The double scroll-shaped straight back is repeated in the legs giving a severe outline to the side view. The invention of such chairs is presumably to be connected with the gradual development of the large dining-table which did not become a regular feature until the mannerist period. At the beginning of the renaissance period, the only type of table was merely a rough oak top laid on wooden trestles, but by the end of the century, tables in Tuscany are known to have had large legs sculpted to reproduce the end section of antique sarcophagi; it was for this that the *sgabello* was designed. However, one very rarely sees a true renaissance table of this type, for most are of a later date with an excess of ornament and with an exaggeration of the carved forms on their legs which places them firmly within the mannerist period. There are also in existence a certain number of smallish, solid hall-tables, supported by a central pedestal, that are stongly reminiscent of Roman stone furniture.

The renaissance bedroom is the most difficult room in a *palazzo* to reconstruct; one wonders what personal comforts the lady of the house gathered around her for the long hours when her husband retreated into his own haven, the *studiolo*. It is interesting to recall that she had no cupboard in which to keep her possessions until the introduction of the *credenza*, or side-cupboard, in the sixteenth century. Until then the *cassone* sufficed. No doubt a loom normally stood by the window; the floors were brightened with rugs and cushions brought back by travellers from the East and the walls were decorated by painted leather 'wallpaper' or by tapestries. The bed, placed on a raised dais, dominated the room; the four-poster, the most imposing type of bed, was, however, less popular than the characteristically Tuscan type with an ornately carved headpiece and four tall twisted columns at each end, surmounted by classical urns carved from wood. (Fig. 6.)

The renowned Lorenzo the Magnificent exemplifies many of the characteristics of the Renaissance and of particular interest is a letter from Lorenzo to his son Giovanni who was then studying in Rome. The letter advises against the tasteless display of wealth in contemporary decoration; a well-ordered and refined household is to be preferred to pomp and display. Much more desirable is the distinction which comes from possessing a few rare antiques (sculpture), and fine books. There is a complete disavowal of interest in contemporary furnishings and the same taste is described in Castiglione's *Il Cortegiano* (English translation, 1561), written in Rome but describing the Court of Federigo da Montefeltro at Urbino – it is a taste which denied decorative excess and demanded the type of well-proportioned, architecturally imposing furniture that has here been described.

Fig. 6 **Bed**, *Tuscan*, c.*1550*. *This type of bed was much more popular than the canopied four-poster; even in their bedrooms, the Florentines loved to be surrounded by ornate carving and lavish gilding.* (*Palazzo Davanzati.*)

6

Pucciarelli

7

Museum Photo

Fig. 7 **Savonarola, or folding X-chair,** *Florentine*, c.*1550*. *Carved oak.* (*Victoria and Albert Museum.*)

8

J. Freeman

Fig. 8 **The Nervi Cassone,** *Florentine, late-fifteenth century. This piece illustrates the renaissance* cassone *at its best. It is exquisitely proportioned and the painted panels are obviously the work of a skilled craftsman.* (*Courtauld Institute Galleries, London.*)

9

Fig. 9 ***Table top*** *inlaid with* pietre dure, *or semi-precious stones, designed by Ligozzi and Poccetti, Florence, 1633–49. This fine example of* pietre dure *contains agates, jaspers, lapis lazuli and chalcedonies on a black marble ground. It was designed for Ferdinando II de' Medici.* *(Museo dell' Opificio delle Pietre Dure, Florence.)*

MUSEUMS AND COLLECTIONS

Collections of Renaissance Furniture are on view at the following:

Amsterdam:	Rijksmuseum
Florence:	Museo Horne Museo Nazionale (Bargello) Palazzo Davanzati Palazzo Vecchio
London:	Courtauld Institute Galleries Victoria and Albert Museum
New York:	Metropolitan Museum of Art
Paris:	Louvre Musée des Arts Décoratifs

FURTHER READING

A History of Italian Furniture from the Fourteenth Century to the early Nineteenth Century by W. Odom, New York, 1966.
World Furniture, ed. by H. Hayward, London, 1965.
Mobili Italiani del Rinascimento by E. Bacchieschi, Milan, 1964.
Furniture and Interior Decoration of the Italian Renaissance by F. Schottmüller, New York, 1928.

16th CENTURY ITALIAN MAIOLICA

In the attempt to imitate Chinese porcelain and Moorish lustreware, the Italians evolved a distinctive and very beautiful form of pottery known as maiolica.

Jock Palmer

J. Freeman

Fig. 1 ***Vase** from Deruta, c.1515. Height 15⅜ ins. The shape is typical of Deruta maiolica, as is the multicoloured decoration. (Victoria and Albert Museum, London.)*

Maiolica is the name given to a distinctive type of Italian pottery with painted decoration on a white glaze containing tin oxide. As early as the fourteenth century, Italian potters were making maiolica painted in a limited range of colours and by the end of the fifteenth century the vogue for these wares, chiefly as decorative objects, was well established, the chief centre of production being Faenza. At first the word maiolica was used only to describe the lustre-decorated pottery imported from Spain in the fourteenth and fifteenth centuries. This was carried in trading ships from Majorca, and the term maiolica is derived from the name of that island. It continued to be used only for lustred wares during the sixteenth century and not until much later was it generally applied to all Italian tin-glazed pottery. The technique of lustre-painting was not discovered in Italy until about 1500, when it was first used at Deruta, near Perugia.

Much of our knowledge of the technical aspects of making maiolica has been obtained from a manuscript entitled *The Three Books of the Potter's Art* (Fig. 6), written by Cipriano Piccolpasso sometime between 1556 and 1559 and now in the Victoria and Albert Museum. Piccolpasso was a native of Castel Durante, a town famous for producing fine maiolica at the beginning of the sixteenth century, but already on the decline by Piccolpasso's time. His manuscript provides not only a full account of the actual processes of manufacture, but also much information about the building of kilns and the recipes for the glazes and pigments. He even explains the best way to make brushes for the painters. Many of the expressions used to describe the manufacture and decoration of maiolica are derived from Piccolpasso, although he uses the word itself to refer to lustre.

Piccolpasso begins with advice on the collection of suitable clay and the preparation of a uniform plastic mass ready to be used by the potter. Round objects were thrown on a wheel, but, if some other shape was required, it was made by pressing slabs of clay into a mould. Tiles and panels were made by cutting slabs of clay to the required shape and thickness. The vessel was then fired in a kiln to produce the so-called biscuit condition, which varied in colour from red to buff.

It was impossible for the painter to erase any mistakes

The next stage was the application of the tin-glaze, the *bianco*, which contained oxides of tin and lead, and *mazacotto*; this last ingredient was made by fusing a mixture of sand and wine lees. The glaze was mixed with water to a milky consistency and the vessel dipped in it. The white coat was allowed to dry and was then ready to be decorated. The surface of this unfired glaze acted rather like blotting-paper and absorbed the pigment immediately it was

16th century
Italian Maiolica

Fig. 2 **Salt-cellar**, c.1580–1600. *Height 9 ins. This appears to be a commemorative piece with the bust of a soldier painted in the well and a Latin inscription referring to his ability to defeat the foe.*
(Victoria and Albert Museum.)

Fig. 3 ***Dish*** *by Maestro Giorgio Andreoli, Gubbio, signed and dated 1527. Diameter 8 ins. The centre is decorated with the arms of Vitelli. The red is produced by the use of copper and is characteristic of pottery from Gubbio.*
(Victoria and Albert Museum.)

2

J. Freeman

3

6

K. Hodle

7

Fig. 4 **Plate** *painted by Nicola Pellipario, Castel Durante, c.1519. Diameter 11⅞ ins. This plate, from the service made for the wife of the Duke of Mantua, depicts the story of Peleus and Thetis. (Fitzwilliam Museum, Cambridge.)*

Fig. 5 ***Inkstand,*** *Urbino, 1550–60. Height 14¾ ins. This highly decorative inkstand illustrates the inventiveness of potters from Urbino. (Victoria and Albert Museum.)*

Fig. 6 *Illustrations from* **Three Books of the Potter's Art** *by Cipriano Piccolpasso, c.1556–59. The kiln is being stoked by assistants while the master supervises the operation. (Victoria and Albert Museum.)*

Museum Photo

J. Freeman

Art-Wood Photography

Fig. 7 **Plate,** *Cafaggiolo, c.1510. Diameter 9¼ ins. The decoration shows a maiolica painter at work with his paints beside him. (Victoria and Albert Museum.)*

applied, making it impossible for the painter to erase any mistakes. But the great advantage of the tin-glaze was that it did not run during the firing.

At the end of the fifteenth century, potters were brought from Montelupo to work for a branch of the Medici family at Cafaggiolo, near Florence. The plate in Fig. 7 comes from this factory and was made there in about 1510. It is attributed to a painter who signed himself Jacopo, and it shows a maiolica painter at work. On a ledge in front of him are two finished pieces and on a bench beside him are his colours in small dishes, each with its own brushes. The maiolica painter by this time had a much wider range of colours, all derived from metallic pigments – blue, yellow, green, purple, orange and occasionally a bright red. A mixture of these produced black; white was obtained from a pigment similar to the *bianco*. By blending these colours he could increase the range.

'Prayers were offered to God with all the heart and the fires were lit'

When the pigments had dried the vessel was given a final transparent lead glaze, the *coperta*, to enhance the brilliance of the colours. The pieces were stacked into the kiln, and then, as Piccolpasso tells us, 'prayers were offered to God with all the heart and the fires were lit'.

For pieces that were to be decorated with lustre, there was still one more stage in the process. The lustre consists of a very thin layer of metal, deposited when the pigment is subjected to a reducing atmosphere in the kiln, at a much lower temperature. The two lustre pigments used in Italy contained either silver or copper. The silver lustre is a rather hard, bright yellow and is typical of Deruta pieces (Fig. 11). Copper produces a glowing ruby red which is characteristic of the pottery of Gubbio (Fig. 3). The most famous of the lustre workshops in Gubbio was that of Maestro Giorgio Andreoli, whose signature, often accompanied by the date, appears on many pieces between the years 1518 and 1541. The dish in Fig. 3 is signed by him and dated 1527 in lustre on the back.

Maiolica was used to make a wide variety of objects and lists of these appear in Piccolpasso's manuscript. Throughout the sixteenth century the emphasis was directed more and more on their decorative qualities, but at all times simple useful wares continued to be made. Among the commonest surviving shapes are plates and dishes, which provided a good surface for the painter to work on. Jugs and vases are found in different sizes and shapes and a group of very large jugs made in the early part of the century has been attributed to Cafaggiolo. The vase in Fig. 1 is a shape characteristic of Deruta and is found with both lustre and polychrome decoration. One important group of maiolica vessels is those made as storage jars for use in pharmacies. The containers for liquids are either long-necked flasks or globular jars with a spout and a handle, while dry drugs were kept in a tall narrow-waisted jar called an *albarello*. The *albarello* in Fig. 12 is attributed to Siena where maiolica was first made at the end of the fifteenth century under the influence of Faenza.

As the century progressed, shapes became more and more complicated and influenced by metalwork. The Faenza dish in Fig. 14, which was made in about 1530, has gadrooning in imitation of a metal piece. At the same time, the decoration took less and less account of the shape or use of the vessel. There is a large table cistern in the Fitzwilliam Museum that is typical of the elaborate shapes of the second half of the century with no area left free of decoration. This was probably made in the Urbino workshop of the Fontana family.

Throughout the sixteenth century the fashion for a particular type of decoration, once established by one centre, was soon taken up at others. This, coupled with the fact that potters and painters moved from place to place, makes the attribution of many pieces to a workshop or even to a particular town very difficult.

16th century
Italian Maiolica

Fig. 8 **Dish depicting Horatio defending the bridge** *painted by Francesco Xanto Avelli, Urbino, 1537. Diameter $18\frac{1}{4}$ ins. (Fitzwilliam Museum.)*

Fig. 9 **Plate** *from Deruta, c.1525. Diameter $14\frac{1}{2}$ ins. (Victoria and Albert Museum.)*

8

Museum Photo

9

Museum Photo

Fig. 10 **Dish** *from Urbino, c.1560–70. $26\frac{1}{2}$ x $20\frac{3}{4}$ ins. In the centre is a scene depicting the gathering of manna while around the borders the delicately painted decoration is reminiscent of antique grotesques. (Victoria and Albert Museum.)*

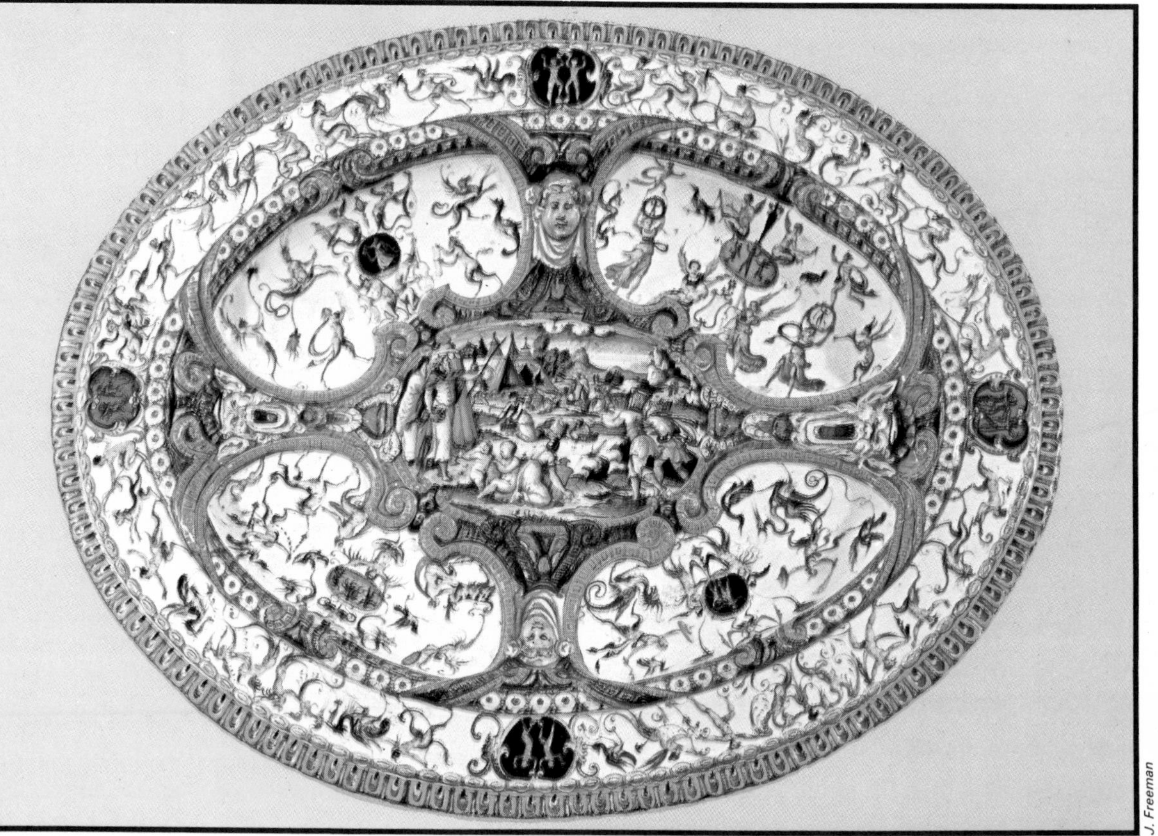

J. Freeman

Fig. 11 **Dish** *from Deruta, early sixteenth century. Diameter $15\frac{1}{2}$ ins. Characteristic of Deruta maiolica decoration is the portrait bust painted in the centre of the plate. (Wallace Collection, London.)*

Fig. 12 **Albarello** *from Siena, c.1500. Height $5\frac{1}{2}$ ins.* Albarelli, *or tall jars with nipped waists, were generally used by apothecaries to hold dry drugs. (Victoria and Albert Museum.)*

11

Museum Photo

12

J. Freeman

13

Fig. 13 **Globular jar** *from Faenza, c.1500. Height $13\frac{1}{2}$ ins. Faenza was the chief centre of production of maiolica during the fifteenth century. This jar has the cherub head and wings pattern repeated around its surface divided up by varied bands of decoration on an ochre ground. The freer, more elegant manner points the way to designs used after 1500. (Gambier-Parry Collection, Courtauld Institute Galleries, London.)*

Museum Photo

14

Fig. 14 **Dish** *from Faenza, c.1530. Diameter 8 ins. The figure of Cupid has always been a popular motif. Here he is shown in a contemplative mood, leaning against an urn. (Victoria and Albert Museum.)*

J. Freeman

The decoration used in the previous century was predominantly concerned with ornamental designs. These patterns based on geometric shapes and plant motifs continued to be used during the early part of the sixteenth century. The large jar attributed to Faenza (Fig. 13) and the Siena *albarello* (Fig. 12) date from about 1500. The decoration on both of them contains elements that were used in the fifteenth century combined in a freer, more elegant manner. On the jar, the decoration in the panels between the cherubs' heads especially, points the way to the designs used after 1500.

The sixteenth century is chiefly noted for the development of a pictorial style of painting known as *istoriato*, in which the decoration represented one or more episodes from a story. These were taken from a great many sources that included the Bible, the works of the writers of antiquity, like Ovid and Pliny, and Italian writers such as Ariosto. For the composition of their designs, the painters made much use of engravings; the print in some cases was copied very closely and in others elements from different prints were combined. Use was also made of woodcut illustrations from early printed books. The Castel Durante plate in Fig. 4 is painted with the story of Peleus and Thetis, adapted from woodcut illustrations in an edition of Ovid's *Metamorphoses*, published in Venice in 1497. By the third decade of the century the principal engravings used were those of Marcantonio Raimondi after the works of Raphael and his School. Because of this, in the late eighteenth century this type of maiolica was associated with Raphael and the ware was called Raphaelle after him. At this time, the practice was begun of identifying the subject of the story on a dish by means of an inscription in blue on the back. This is often accompanied by the date and sometimes by the artist's signature.

The earliest *istoriato* pieces came from Faenza and Cafaggiolo, but it was at Castel Durante and later at Urbino that the style developed. One of the most distinguished of all the *istoriato* painters was Nicola Pellipario. He began his career at Castel Durante where in about 1519 he painted a service for Isabella d'Este, wife of Gianfrancesco Gonzaga, duke of Mantua (Fig. 4). By 1528 he had moved to Urbino and he continued there until the early 1540s. Another well-known painter working in Urbino at the same time was Francesco Xanto Avelli. He painted the large dish in Fig. 8 showing Horatio defending the bridge, taken from Livy's history of Rome. It is inscribed on the back with his signature and the date 1537. During the second half of the century the Fontana workshop introduced a style of decoration using grotesques, based on prints after the frescoes by Raphael in the Vatican (Fig. 10). *Istoriato* ware in the Urbino style was produced in Venice, but the characteristic maiolica of this centre has the tin-glaze stained pale blue, with painting in dark blue and white.

Reaction against this profusion of decoration led to the production of pieces painted with sketchy figures in blue, yellow and orange. Others were left white without any decoration. Both these types continued to be made into the seventeenth century.

MUSEUMS AND COLLECTIONS

Collections of Italian maiolica are represented at the following:

Cambridge:	Fitzwilliam Museum
Edinburgh:	Royal Scottish Museum
Faenza:	Museo Internazionale delle Ceramiche
Florence:	Museo Nazionale (Bargello)
London:	British Museum
	Victoria and Albert Museum
	Wallace Collection
Milan:	Museo Civico
Oxford:	Ashmolean Museum
Rome:	Museo di Palazzo Venezia
Venice:	Civico Museo Correr

FURTHER READING

Five Centuries of Italian Maiolica by Guiseppe Liverani, New York, 1960.

Italian Maiolica by Bernard Rackham, London, 1952.

Catalogue of Italian Maiolica by Bernard Rackham, Victoria and Albert Museum, London, 1940.

The Three Books of the Potter's Art (Li tre libri dell' arte del vasajo) by Cipriano Piccolpasso. Translated by Bernard Rackham and Albert van der Put, London, 1934.

Guide to Italian Maiolica by Bernard Rackham, Victoria and Albert Museum, London, 1933.

Glass-making, the Venetian Monopoly

Sylvia Coppen-Gardner

1

Museum Photo

2

Museum Photo

3

Museum Photo

Fig. 4 ***Hexagonal bottle with threads of milk glass on exterior,*** *Italian, late sixteenth or early seventeenth century. (Museo Vetrario, Murano.)*

Fig. 1 *Illumination from* ***The Travels of Sir John Mandeville*** *(published between 1357 and 1371) illustrating early glass-making, Flemish or German, fifteenth century. (British Museum, London.)*

Fig. 2 ***Green glass enamelled goblet with portrait head in cartouche and gilded foot,*** *Venetian, c.1480. Height 6¾ ins. Early Venetian glass illustrates forcibly the splendours of renaissance Italy. Magnificent gilding and enamelling to resemble gems was common on such goblets which were often made to commemorate a betrothal or marriage. Great artists of the day were sometimes commissioned to decorate these glasses. (Victoria and Albert Museum, London.)*

Fig. 3 ***Enamelled beaker decorated with two Mermen,*** *Venetian, c.1490. Height 5 ins. Renaissance motifs were commonly painted on drinking-glasses, whose basic shapes were often influenced by designs for silver. It was not until the sixteenth century that specific glass shapes were developed. (Victoria and Albert Museum.)*

At a moment when superb skill was turned for the first time to the production of secular objects, glass became one of the most important luxuries.

The glass industry in Europe – for the production of glass other than window glass – began in Venice. The Venetians established a highly developed industry with a vast export trade which virtually dominated the rest of Europe until the middle of the seventeenth century and all subsequent development in European glass stems from the Venetian tradition.

Venice, a great trading nation geographically situated between Western Europe and Asia, with trading stations all over the Near East, had a flourishing glass industry with a considerable trade by the thirteenth century; but Venetian glass is not datable before the fifteenth century. The finest period is from 1500 to 1550.

Venetian, like Roman, glass is a light and thin-walled soda glass, made from raw materials obtained by the Venetians through their trade. It consists of soda ash, imported either from Spain or Egypt, and white pebbles from the Po or the Ticino, together with lime in the form of powdered marble or crushed sea shells to give this very delicate substance added stability. By the end of the tenth century there were probably glass-workers in Venice making simple glass objects such as bottles and flasks, possibly with the help of craftsmen from Byzantium or Syria where there were well-established glass industries at this period.

In the thirteenth century the glass industry became a monopoly of the Venetian Republic and in 1292 the glass-houses were established on the island of Murano, where they still exist today. This move was made not only to avoid the risk of fire in Venice itself, where all glass-houses had to be not less than fifteen paces from any dwelling-place, but also to establish a state industry so rigidly controlled that the establishment of glass-houses elsewhere could be prevented. The Venetian glass-workers were organised in an elaborate guild system and were virtually prisoners of the state, with very restricted freedom of movement. They were forbidden to emigrate from Venice on pain of death. The export of glass-making materials and of cullet, the broken and waste glass, was also forbidden so as to keep the secret of glass-making in Venice. Glass-houses were nonetheless established in Bologna and Ferrara in the thirteenth century, and in the sixteenth and seventeenth centuries there was a widespread establishment of glass-houses on the Venetian pattern elsewhere in Europe.

Early Venetian glass was simple – jugs, carafes and bottles – but in the fifteenth century, with the great impetus of the Renaissance, glass became one of the most splendid and elaborate art forms of the period. Fifteenth-century Venetian glass was heavy and massive in shape, closely influenced by contemporary silver, and it was not only brilliant in colour but also a vehicle for magnificent and grandiose decoration. The splendour of renaissance Italy is illustrated very forcibly in these early pieces of Venetian glass. By the end of the fifteenth century the Venetian glass-workers could produce blue, green, purple and opaque white glass, and the latter was probably used in the first recorded experiment in the making of European porcelain, by Maestro Antonio di San Simone, in 1470. Some of the glass was made in imitation of semi-precious stones, such as onyx, agate and chalcedony (Fig. 5), but the great feature of fifteenth-century Venetian glass is the use of enamelled decoration (Figs. 2 and 6).

Enamelling on glass first appeared in Venice in the mid-fifteenth century. Great use was made of dark backgrounds of coloured glass to display the beauty of the enamel decoration, which was painted in fusible enamel and fired by baking in a small oven. This is an Islamic technique of the thirteenth and fourteenth centuries, but it probably developed independently in Venice from the use of enamel on metalwork. The decoration on enamelled glass had similarities with contemporary renaissance decorative motifs and was used not only in a pictorial fashion but also in coloured spots of enamel, giving a gem-like effect comparable with the decoration on contemporary goldsmiths' work (Fig. 6). It was mainly used, in its pictorial form, for the decoration of goblets and chalices, often commissioned to commemorate a betrothal or a marriage, and there is a very strong influence between this form of decoration and contemporary painting (Fig. 3). Vivarini, the early Venetian painter, probably did some pictorial decoration on glass, but this type of elaborate decoration was comparatively short-lived and in the sixteenth century it rarely appears.

The Venetian glass industry reached its height in the sixteenth century. There was enormous prosperity and the huge export from Venice dominated the rest of Europe. In this period of increased trade and, consequently, of increased wealth, when the ideas of the Renaissance were spreading from Italy to the rest of Europe, glass became not only a highly desirable luxury, but also a great status symbol; the finest pieces were sent from Venice to the princely Courts and rich merchants' houses. A great number of the pieces were not made for practical use, but were collected by connoisseurs and used as

5

J. Freeman

6

Museum Photo

7

Angelo Hornak

8

Angelo Hornak

9

Angelo Hornak

Fig. 5 ***Ewer in imitation chalcedony,*** *Venetian, c.1500. Height 12 ins.*
By the late fifteenth century, Venetian glass-makers had reached a high degree of technical proficiency. They were able to produce many different effects, one of which was the imitation of semi-precious stones such as onyx, agate and chalcedony.
(Victoria and Albert Museum.)

Fig. 6 ***Cup and cover*** *with* ***enamelled decoration,*** *Venetian, late-fifteenth century. Height 18 in.*
Although most fifteenth-century enamelling was done on dark-coloured glass backgrounds, this is a fine example of the use of cristallo.
(Victoria and Albert Museum.)

Fig. 7 ***Nef, or boat-shaped ewer,*** *attributed to Armenia Vivarini, Venetian, mid-sixteenth century. Armenia Vivarini was a descendant of the painter Antonio Vivarini. This piece is typical of the fantastic and elaborate articles which were made in glass in the sixteenth century to grace the tables of the rich throughout Europe.*
(Museo Vetrario.)

Fig. 8 ***Reliquary of*** **cristallo** ***with a high foot sprayed with gold and enamelled decoration,*** *Venetian, late-fifteenth or early-sixteenth century.*
Glass used for religious purposes during the Renaissance followed quite closely the forms of table-glass.
(Museo Vetrario.)

Fig. 9 ***Casket with lid of white net glass,*** *Venetian, mid-sixteenth century.*
Glass-making was at its height in the sixteenth century. Magnificent pieces of vetro de trina *or lace-glass such as this casket were made not just for practical purposes, but for collectors who desired them for their beauty and intricacy. Shapes were devised to show off the material to perfection, as in the knops on the top of this piece.*
(Museo Vetrario.)

display objects by those who wished to emphasise their fashionable taste – and their wealth – in the eyes of society. In the sixteenth century, the increased development in the technical skill of the Venetian glass-workers led to the vast expansion in trade. Shapes specifically suitable for glass were evolved, and there was less dependence on shapes of metalwork and ceramics, as previously.

Venetian glass of the sixteenth century is fanciful and fantastic, much lighter in design and far less massive in shape and size than glass of the fifteenth century. A glass similar in appearance to rock crystal, called *cristallo*, one of the most prized objects of the century, was created and became immediately fashionable. There was very little surface decoration and use of coloured glass at this period. What enamelled decoration there was, was carried out on a clear ground and was mostly made for the export market. Glass objects appear in Venetian paintings, showing the luxury and splendour of Venetian life. Mirror glasses were also made from the beginning of the century and a French traveller in 1584 writes of glass musical instruments.

The *cristallo* developed in Venice in the sixteenth century was probably discovered about 1450 and was often tinged with a pale grey colour. This was dissipated in the sixteenth century by blowing the glass more thinly. Refined by the use of manganese, *cristallo* was the most famous glass made in Venice and was not allowed to be sold by pedlars or by stall-holders. It is mentioned as being displayed by the glass-workers at the Ascension Day Fair in Saint Mark's Square.

An air of fantasy in keeping with contemporary design

Venetian *cristallo* was so fragile that it could not be refired for decorative purposes because of the risk of distortion and so, in the sixteenth century, a great emphasis was placed upon elaborate shapes and upon decorative borders, stems and handles, applied to the glass itself. The only other form of decoration to be used was diamond-point engraving – never very popular in Venice and rarely figurative, as in English glass of the period – and some fine applied gilding. *Cristallo* was used to great effect to create fantastic and elaborate articles, such as the magnificent *nefs*, or boat-shaped ewers, which graced the tables of renaissance Europe (Fig. 7). Objects such as these were highly desirable, not only for their beauty, but also for their originality and for their air of fantasy which is very much in keeping with contemporary design.

The Venetians also produced *latticinio* (reticulated, filigree or lace-glass), first mentioned in its most elaborate form in 1540. This is glass with the incorporation of an opaque or coloured glass thread used in the metal and it involves a highly complicated and difficult process. In its most complex form, as *vetro de trina*, or lace-glass (Venice had a world-famous lace industry), it was evolved to produce fantastic and elaborate objects for the purpose of display (Fig 9), but it was also used, in its simpler form as a common type of decoration in glass in the late sixteenth and early seventeenth centuries (Fig. 4).

Another elaborate form of glass which appears in sixteenth-century Venice is ice-glass, or crackle-glass, which first appeared in the middle of the century and which was a very short-lived fashion.

The discovery of the trade route to the East by Vasco da Gama in 1497–98 had a long term effect on Venetian trade generally. With the rise of other glass industries in Europe, Venice was beginning to decline as the paramount influence upon European glass by the end of the sixteenth century. As early as the mid-fifteenth century a serious rival industry had appeared at L'Altare, near Genoa. Glass-workers from Normandy had established a glass-workers' guild there to spread the secret of the craft and to establish new glass-houses. Their wares were similar in type and style to Venetian glass. Throughout the sixteenth century Venetian domination was constantly being eroded by the proliferation of glass-houses making Venetian-inspired glass, the most important being that of Antwerp, founded by Venetian workmen in 1541.

It is in the development of drinking-glasses that Venice had her greatest and most long-lasting influence. The shapes, developed from the early beakers and goblets, had a profound effect upon the glass that was made outside Murano until the middle of the seventeenth century, when individual national styles began to appear. The exaggerated shapes of the stems of Venetian glasses, the moulded baluster-stems of the sixteenth century and the seventeenth-century winged stems with their elaborate trailed decoration, in particular, had enormous influence.

MUSEUMS AND COLLECTIONS

Collections of Italian glass are on view at the following:

Birmingham:	Art Gallery
Cologne:	Kunstgewerbemuseum
London:	British Museum Victoria and Albert Museum
Munich:	Bayerisches National-museum
New York:	Corning Glass Museum Metropolitan Museum of Art
Paris:	Musée du Petit Palais
Prague:	Museum of Decorative Art
St. Helen's:	Pilkington Glass Museum
Vienna:	Österreichisches Museum für Angewandte Kunst
West Berlin:	Kunstgewerbemuseum

It is also possible to visit the factories in Murano, to watch the manufacture of modern Venetian glass. The factories are usually open every day except Sunday.

FURTHER READING

Masterpieces of Glass, British Museum, London, 1968. The catalogue for the 8th International Congress of Glass held at the British Museum.
Italian Blown Glass from Ancient Rome to Venice, by G. Mariacher, London, 1961.
Glass, by W. B. Honey, Victoria and Albert Museum Handbook I, London, 1946.

PAPER-KNIVES

From the middle of the seventeenth century onwards the dagger fell increasingly into disuse. Since the business of raising seals or cutting open letters demanded considerable delicacy, it was not long before a new kind of knife was developed expressly for this purpose. In the eighteenth century paper-knives were often of exquisite workmanship. In Germany the Solingen sword manufacturers produced miniature rapiers and sabres for use as paper-knives, a tradition which was carried on until the last war. In south Germany and Italy paper-knives also tended to be small-scale reproductions of fighting weapons, finely chiselled and handsomely ornamented. In France and Britain, however, paper-knives evolved in new forms. Increasing contact with India and the Far East led to the introduction of new design motifs in England. Ivory knives containing carved figures of Indian gods and elephants were popular and, during the Napoleonic Wars, knives bearing the portraits or busts of military and naval heroes were made cheaply. The French specialised in fine enamelled hilts as did the Dutch and to a lesser extent the Germans.

The Victorian era saw a great proliferation in the making of paper-knives; horn, jet and ceramics of all kinds were used and, by the end of the century, embossed and decorated metal knives became popular. The design of paper-knives has scarcely altered since that time, although simpler shapes predominate.

Collecting Hints

Paper-knives from the eighteenth century and earlier are unlikely to appear on the market in that guise; they will be listed for their enamelling or craftsmanship. It is easy to pick up Victorian paper-knives cheaply.

Far left: ***Paper-knife.*** *Tortoise-shell with silver handle. £8.50.*

Middle left: ***Paper-knife.*** *Silver with a decorative bear handle. £3.50.*

Left: ***Paper-knife.*** *Horn with a silver handle.*

Below: ***Paper-knife*** *commemorating Queen Victoria's Diamond Jubilee, 1897.*

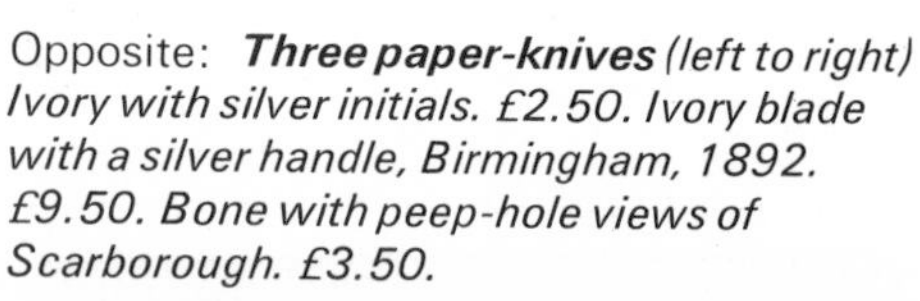

Opposite: ***Three paper-knives*** *(left to right) Ivory with silver initials. £2.50. Ivory blade with a silver handle, Birmingham, 1892. £9.50. Bone with peep-hole views of Scarborough. £3.50.*

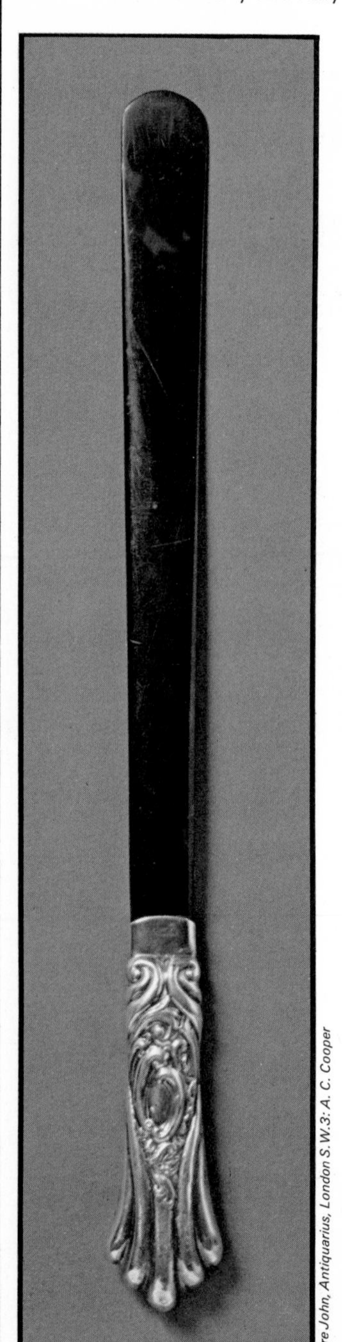

Guinevere John, Antiquarius, London S.W.3: A. C. Cooper

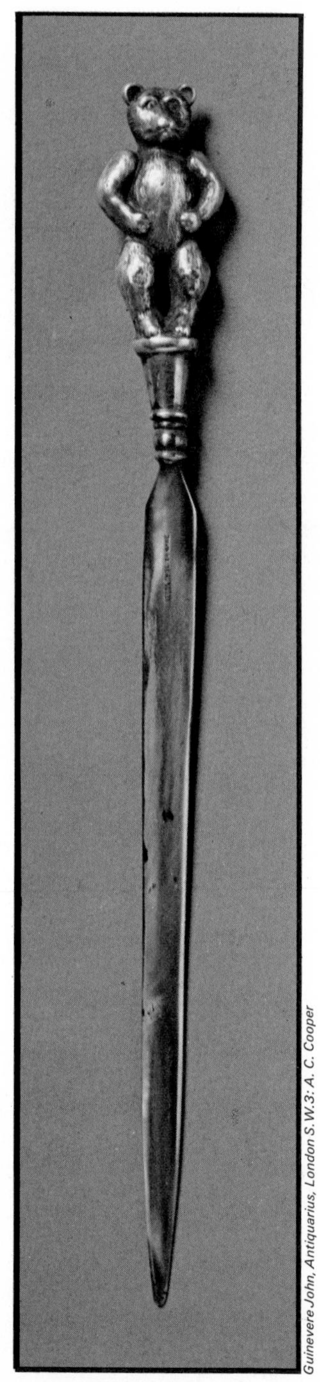

Guinevere John, Antiquarius, London S.W.3: A. C. Cooper

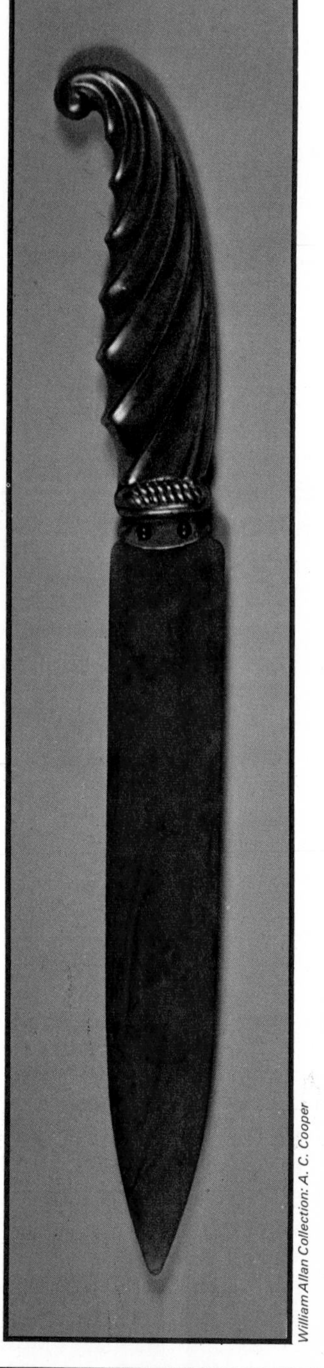

William Allan Collection: A. C. Cooper

Philippa Lewis Collection: A. C. Cooper

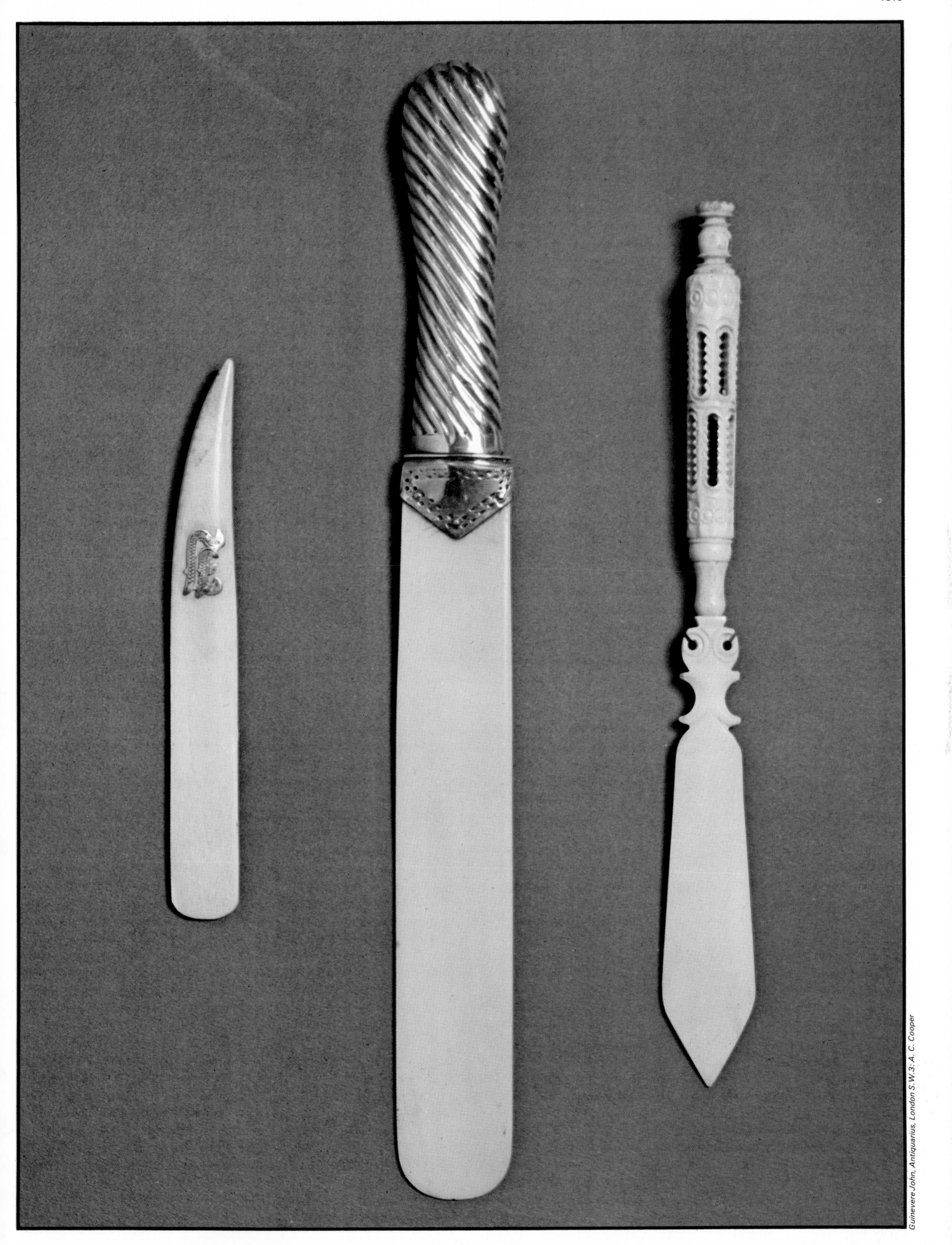

Guinevere John, Antiquarius, London S.W.3: A. C. Cooper

RENAISSA TREASUR

The renaissance craftsmen avished their skills upon beautiful pronze statuettes, cameos of ivory and semi-precious stone, vases of gold and silver and nautilus shells. These were the collectors' pieces n an age of extravagance. Their creators sought to emulate the treasures of classical antiquity, matching fine workmanship with an understanding of the character of their materials.

'ig. 1 **Shouting Warrior on Horseback** by Riccio died 1532), *c.*1510. Bronze, height 13½ ins.
Andrea Briosco, known as Riccio or curly-head, vas probably the greatest exponent of the art of he bronze statuette. His early apprenticeship as a goldsmith in Padua combined with later sculpture raining in Florence to give him a complete command of the techniques of metal-working and a ure grasp of sculptural form, to which he added his own compassionate vision. Not content merely to produce decorative objects, he used the medium as a vehicle for expressive works of art, such as this penetrating study of the stress of battle, which possesses on a tiny scale scarcely less authority han the great equestrian monuments of the time. Victoria and Albert Museum, London.)

'ig. 2 **Meleager** by Antico (died 1528), late ifteenth century. Bronze, partially gilt, inlaid with silver, height 12 ins.
A complete contrast with the bronzes of Riccio is provided by those of his contemporary Pier Jacopo Alari Bonacolsi, known as Antico because of his devotion to antique models. Antico spent his life n the service of the Gonzaga, the ruling family of Mantua, and this bronze was made for his first patron Gianfrancesco Gonzaga. It is typical of his work, first in its close dependence upon a classical marble, which was in the Uffizi until its destruction by fire in the eighteenth century, and secondly in its sumptuousness of execution with silver-inlaid eyes and teeth and gilded hair, moustache and clothing, which make it into a superb decorative object.
Victoria and Albert Museum, London.)

NCE

ES

Fig. 3 **Apollo** by Giovanni Bologna (1529–1608), 1575. Bronze, height 34½ ins.
In 1570 the apartments of Francesco de' Medici in the Palazzo Vecchio were redesigned by Vasari. The most remarkable of these rooms is the *studiolo*, the decoration of which was designed to represent the Elements. Panel paintings cover the walls, and above these are eight niches filled with a series of bronze statuettes by the leading sculptors in Florence at the time, providing a conspectus of contemporary sculpture. The most original of these statuettes is this figure of Apollo, representing Fire, by the Flemish sculptor Giovanni Bologna, who settled in Florence. It is no exaggeration to say he produced a new style which was to change the face of European sculpture.
(Palazzo Vecchio, Florence.)

3

Fig. 4 **Shepherd Milking a Goat** by Riccio, early sixteenth century. Bronze, height $10\frac{1}{4}$ ins.
This statuette is perhaps more typical of Riccio than his shouting horseman (Fig. 1). Riccio was a close friend of the humanist academics of the University of Padua and for them he created in his statuettes a vision of the arcadian world of classical mythology, peopled with satyrs, nymphs, shepherds and goats. This beautiful bronze testifies to his thorough grasp of classical form. It was made to stand beside actual classical bronzes in the study of a learned Paduan collector and it became sufficiently famous to be reproduced in 1520 by the painter Falconetto in a fresco-cycle in the neighbouring city of Mantua.
(Museo Nazionale (Bargello), Florence.)

Fig. 5 **Neptune** by Alessandro Vittoria (1525–1608), *c.*1580–85. Bronze, height $19\frac{1}{2}$ ins.
Alessandro Vittoria was the most important sculptor working in Venice in the latter part of the sixteenth century. Although his major work was in marble, he was also the author of a large number of beautiful bronze statuettes. This remarkable bronze, which represents Neptune stilling the waves to protect the Trojan fleet, may be seen as a sculptural counterpart of the muscular nudes of Vittoria's contemporary, Tintoretto; the poses of the human figure and the sea-horse have been violently twisted to wring the maximum in opposed tensions from the composition. Unlike the fluent figures of Giovanni Bologna (Fig. 3), it carries a tremendous emotional charge. (Victoria and Albert Museum, London.)

4

Bertoni

5

G. Rainbird

Fig. 6 **Ceremonial Jubilee Hammer,** bearing the arms of Pope Julius III (1487–1555), Italian, *c.*1550. This superb Jubilee hammer is one of the most beautiful known examples of renaissance metalwork. There are no records as to its authorship, but it must have been made by a goldsmith with an expert's knowledge of die-cutting, since the technical aspects of the work are as astounding as the artistic quality. While no definite attribution can be made, both the design and the workmanship are on a level with those of Benvenuto Cellini, the greatest goldsmith of his age.
Jubilee hammers were used by the Pope during his jubilee year *(jubileum)*, which occurred only every twenty-five years and included the ceremonial opening of the doors of St. Peter's in Rome. This particular hammer was commissioned by Paul III (1468–1549), who was a member of the Farnese family, pope from 1534 until his death, and the instigator of the Counter-Reformation. He died, however, before the jubilee year of 1550. The hammer, which must have been nearly complete at the time of his death, was passed on to his successor. Julius III, who took over the Papacy in 1550 and served until 1555; he evidently had his arms engraved on to the hammer, but he can have had little to do with the actual making of the piece.
(Bayerisches Nationalmuseum, Munich.)

Fig. 7 **Hercules and the Hydra** by Antico, early sixteenth century. Bronze, partially gilt, diameter $12\frac{3}{4}$ ins.
In about 1500 Antico entered the service of the famous Isabella d'Este, the wife of Francesco Gonzaga, Marquis of Mantua, for whom he was to produce much of his finest work in bronze. Isabella commissioned in honour of her father Ercole I d'Este, Duke of Ferrara, a series of bronze roundels depicting the Labours of Hercules. Five of this series exist, divided between London and Vienna, while especially finely worked duplicates of two of the Labours, of which this is one, are preserved in Florence. They are traceable to the collection of the d'Este family and were thus almost certainly made by Antico for Duke Ercole himself to the order of Isabella.
(Museo Nazionale (Bargello), Florence.)

Scala

Scala

Scala

Scala

M. Desjardines Realities

Fig. 8 **Oval vase** by Bernardo Buontalenti (1536–1608), 1583, the mounts by Giacomo Bilivert. Lapis lazuli mounted in gold, height 16 ins.
Carved in the base are the Medici arms, the initials F.M. and the date 1583, which indicate that the vase was commissioned by Francesco I de' Medici.
(Museo degli Argenti, Florence.)

Fig. 9 **Flask** of double shell form, Milanese, possibly by Jacopo da Trezzo (1570–80). Spanish jasper mounted in gold, enamel and pearls, height $10\frac{7}{8}$ ins.
(Museo degli Argenti, Florence.)

Fig. 10 **Cameo depicting Cosimo I de' Medici with his wife, Eleanora of Toledo, and their children** by Giovanni Antonio de' Rossi (1517–*c.* 1575), 1557–62. White onyx on a chalcedony ground, height $7\frac{3}{8}$ ins.
Cosimo I commissioned Rossi to carve this exquisite work in 1557, and paid him 200 ducats at the time. Rossi worked on it for three years in Florence, then returned to Rome to continue the work. In March 1562, Cosimo's ambassador in Rome, Minali, sent word home that it would be finished by the following June, and assured him that it was 'one of the rarest things to be seen in the world today'. Vasari wrote of the piece in 1568 and is reputed to have made the drawing of it which is now in Christ Church Library, Oxford. It must indeed have been a magnificent object complete with its representation of Florence in the central hollow.
(Museo degli Argenti, Florence.)

Fig. 11 **Vase in the shape of a Hydra,** topped by a figure of Hercules. Jasper mounted in gold and pearls, height $13\frac{3}{8}$ ins.
Previously attributed to the great Flemish sculptor Giovanni da Bologna, this beautiful vase is now thought to be in the Milanese tradition. In 1581, one Michele Mazzafirri was paid fifty *scudi* by the Grand Duke Francesco I to create two 'Labours of Hercules' and it seems likely that this vase is one of the pieces to which records refer.
(Museo degli Argenti, Florence.)

Fig. 12 **Nautilus shell,** mounted in silver-gilt, Italian, first half of the sixteenth century. Throughout Europe in the sixteenth century, rare objects were mounted in silver for protection and decoration. Coconut shells, ostrich eggs and pieces of prized china were treated in this way as well as more delicate sea shells. The decorative motifs on this lovely example are typical of this sort of work: the tortoise and diminutive Neptune were used on English and German pieces as well. The tiger-skin effect of the shell itself is distinctively Italian; it has been left in its natural state instead of being polished white like northern examples.
(Museo Lázaro Galdiano, Madrid.)

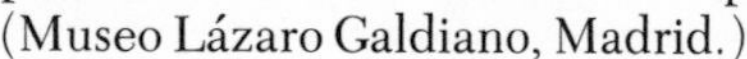

High Baroque Interiors

Martin Meade

The achievements of the Baroque, both practical and intellectual, set the seal on the triumph of the Counter-Reformation.

Fig. 1 (frontispiece) ***Farnese Gallery**, Rome, decorated by Annibale and Agostino Carracci, 1597–1604.*
Illustrating the Triumph of Love, this decoration is the earliest and one of the most magnificent baroque interiors.

Fig. 2 **Gran Salone,** *Stupinigi, by Filippo Juvarra (1678–1736), begun 1719.*
Stupinigi is unquestionably Juvarra's masterpiece. The style represents the synthesis of the Baroque – a style which had by this time become international.

The term 'Baroque' once had a derogatory connotation, implying an excessive extravagance of shape and a super-abundance of florid decoration. The term is now used, however, as an accepted description of the arts of the seventeenth century in general and in particular those of Italy in that century. The characteristics are a dominant sense of mass coupled with a feeling for movement and complex spatial relationships, with a wealth of decoration binding the whole.

By the late sixteenth century, Mannerism seemed to have reached an *impasse* with an over-conscious seeking for originality, variety and caprice on the one hand and an arid deliberate classicism on the other, though such outstanding figures as Tintoretto and Correggio, Palladio and Michelangelo transcended the stereotyped formulae by their individual genius.

2

Scala

From the turn of the century to about 1620 must be considered the period of transition in the baroque style. Official taste – that of the Papal Court – remained largely faithful to late Mannerism, but at the same time a number of enlightened patrons collected and encouraged the new style. The wind of change blew from the north of Italy. As in the sixteenth century, so in the seventeenth, there were few Romans amongst the great men of Rome.

From Bologna came Annibale Carracci (1560–1609) with his brother Agostino, and soon afterwards a whole group of artists well versed in the techniques of fresco painting. They were to establish themselves as the most active group of decorators in Rome at the beginning of the century, thanks to the patronage of such powerful figures as Cardinal Odoardo Farnese and Pope Gregory XV, who was himself from Bologna.

The *saloni*, or grand reception rooms, of the baroque palaces were vast. Flat ceilings were common, but increasingly the barrel-vault predominated, its decoration eventually covering the whole surface. The Mannerists had often broken with the renaissance framework of pilasters and cornices for the walls, but the artists of the Baroque were to return to this method and elaborate it. One innovation of later sixteenth century planning that did continue, however, was the emphasis on the gallery as the most sumptuous room in the palace.

The expansion of real into imaginary space

In 1597 Annibale Carracci received the commission for the decoration of the vault of the gallery in the Farnese Palace (Fig. 1), designed by Vignola in the 1560s. The walls were painted in gold and white forming a striking contrast to the colour of the ceiling. Annibale's scheme for the barrel-vault involved a novel continuity of the architectural framework of the room into the painted decoration of the ceiling. Illusionistic architectural painting, creating an expansion of real into imaginary space, had already been employed in the High Renaissance. It really came into its own, however, in the latter part of the sixteenth century – particularly in Bologna, where it would have been well known to Annibale.

He did not, however, make use of a purely illusionistic technique in the execution of his decorative mythological programme, of which the theme was to be *The Triumph of Love*. The main scenes are framed as easel paintings, the illusionistic architecture and decoration appearing to continue behind them. The decorative effect is enhanced by simulated plaster-work (stucco) figures in front of which recline or sit male nudes painted as if they were flesh and blood. The contrast of this 'real' background and the painted mythological scenes in their gilt frames is, therefore, emphasised and it helps to bind the whole together.

Despite the wealth of overlapping motifs which in mannerist hands would have been ambiguous, the scheme always remains logical with a subtle progression towards the centre which contains the main scene, *The Triumph of Bacchus and Ariadne*. The figures in these vivid mythological stories have a sculptural solidity and have acquired a fluid grace of movement and warmth of colour emphasising the new full-blooded imaginative approach that Annibale brought to the fresco tradition.

The innovations introduced by the Carracci and their school were quickly followed by similar developments in architecture. Carlo Maderno (1556–1629) was the first architect to break with the austerity and ambiguity of mannerist buildings, introducing a sculptural boldness and clarity that had been lost for a number of generations. His façade for the church of Sta. Susanna (1603) (Fig. 6) and his nave and façade of St. Peter's (designed 1606, completed 1626) show a lucid progression of the decorative elements towards the centre. The sculptural quality of each element, whether column, pilaster or niche, is boldly individualised without detracting from the strong horizontal and vertical flow of movement in the façade.

The Palazzo Barberini has an open façade with wings projecting from the main block. A type which up till then is only found in the villas around Rome was now drawn out of the seclusion of its grounds to confront the *gravitas* of the Roman scene. The centre block is majestically articulated by three arcaded stories of almost equal value, the ground floor being opened as a wide loggia. Here one finds a development of the airy spaciousness of the Genoese palaces and villas with their loggias and amply columned courtyards.

The Palazzo Barberini was begun in 1628, but Maderno died in the course of the following year and the architect appointed to continue his work was Gianlorenzo Bernini (1598–1680) with the assistance of Francesco Borromini (1599–1667), who was to be responsible for some of the decorative detail.

These two men together with Pietro da Cortona (1596–1669) were to be the creative giants of their age: the High Baroque. They brought an all-encompassing breadth of vision to their art. Cortona was not only an architect but a brilliant artist and decorator as well, having immense fresco commissions in hand concurrently with his architectural projects. Borromini was the more introspective character, but his disturbing, fascinating work is in many ways the more original. A late starter, he was a jealous rival of Bernini, who, for more than half a century, was to dominate the artistic life of Italy, centred on Rome.

3

Courtauld Institute of Art

Fig. 3 ***Drawing of the Scala Regia,*** *Vatican, built by Bernini (1598–1680), 1663–66. Bernini's last great work, the Scala Regia clearly illustrates his ingenuity and outstanding ability to turn a difficult site to his advantage. By diminishing the size of the columns as they recede and by placing them closer to the wall, the fact that the space is greatly narrowed at the top is not noticed by the spectator.*

Bernini surpassed even Michelangelo in the adaptability of his skills

Bernini was a universal genius, combining the talents primarily of a sculptor with those of painter and architect, stage designer and playwright, as well as poet, surpassing even Michelangelo in the adaptability of his skills.

The Papal Court was now once again the discerning centre of patronage for the most distinguished artists of the time. It was Urban VIII Barberini (1623–44) who handed over to Bernini on the death of Maderno the commission for the completion of his *palazzo*. Not only was he a patron, but a life-long friend and admirer. On the day of his elevation to the papacy he is supposed to have called Bernini to him saying, 'Your luck is great to see Cardinal Maffeo Barberini Pope, Cavalieri, but ours is much greater to have Cavalieri Bernini alive in our Pontificate'.

To his architecture and planning he brought the vigour and feeling for spatial movement found in his sculpture. The general conception of the Barberini palace façade was Maderno's, but Bernini enriched the sculptural value of the columns and pilasters on each floor. Internally, the main staircase is wider and more open than was previously common in Rome, a fulfilment of Vasari's declaration, 'Let the stairs be grand in every way, for many see the stairs and nothing more of the house'. The second oval staircase is, however, a Palladian motif. This is expanded in spatial movement with the concavity of the central niche in the columned entrance hall, leading to an oval saloon, a plan that must owe something as well to the ruins of classical Rome.

His sense of scale and movement coupled with great ingenuity can be seen in a late work of 1663–66: the Scala Regia in the Vatican. (Fig. 3.) Here Bernini had to provide a grand access for the Pope from his palace to St. Peter's. The site was a constricted one and the stairs had to be fitted in at right angles to the church. The space allowed for was narrow and long, the walls converging towards

Fig. 4 ***The Sleeping Diana** by Pietro da Cortona (1596–1669), lunette in the Pitti Palace, Florence, 1640s.*
Cortona's work in the Pitti Palace is not illusionistic and pictorial space is clearly defined. The exuberant richness of the ornament, however, is equalled only by the exquisite quality of Cortona's brushwork.

Fig. 5 ***Dome of S. Carlo alle Quattro Fontane**, Rome, by Francesco Borromini (1599–1667), 1638–46.*
At S. Carlo, Borromini, the most original genius of the Italian Baroque, produced one of the most ingenious spatial compositions ever designed. Completely disregarding convention, the walls undulate with a swaying rhythm creating an ever-moving, sculpturally voluptuous effect. The whole plan is steadied by the firm oval of the dome which appears to rise steeply towards the lantern, an illusion created by the diminishing size of the honeycomb pattern.

the upper end. To counteract the narrowing effect, Bernini used a tunnel-shaped roof supported by columns which diminish in size and stand nearer to the wall towards the top. The dramatic use of lighting also helps to conceal the difficulties involved and highlights the drama of the ascent.

His understanding of scenic possibilities was brought to bear in his religious work, which set the seal on the triumph of the Counter-Reformation. The Cornaro Chapel of 1645–52 is a brilliant combination of all possible techniques used to draw the attention of the spectator to his marble sculpture, the *Ecstasy of St. Teresa.* The daring illusionism of the Chapel was, in fact, too extreme to set a precedent in Rome. But its interpenetration of the real and unreal was to be taken up with fervour in the late baroque development of Spain, Portugal and especially Germany.

He was received as the premier artist of his age

Such was Bernini's international fame, that the 'Sun King' of France, Louis XIV, begged him to come to Paris to present new designs for the enlargement of the Louvre. He was received with all the honours due to the premier artist of his age but the projects were on too vast and formal a scale in their internal arrangements and out of sympathy with French taste. However, such features as the projected two-storied oval hall as a setting for court life, and the giant order used to articulate the elevations, were to have very important repercussions in later baroque planning and design.

The major palace completed by Bernini was the Chigi-Odescalchi, where the giant order propounded for the Louvre was carried out. It was this palace front, with its order rising from the first floor containing its suite of grand reception rooms, its balustraded parapet crowned by statues completing the vertical elements of the design and the lower rusticated wings, that was to become a model for palaces of the nobility all over Europe.

The glamour, fame and extrovert personality of Bernini

The career of Francesco Borromini is strongly in contrast with the glamour, fame and extrovert personality of Bernini. For many years he was employed as a mason and sculptor in St. Peter's. After the death of his relative, Maderno, he continued for a while as assistant to Bernini both in St. Peter's and at the Palazzo Barberini. There, his highly personal manner was already apparent in the second floor windows and in the door surrounds inside the palace where Borromini's freedom of approach would seem to dominate that of Bernini for a while. But the two could not work together for long; their difference in temperament was too great and Bernini's precipitous rise to fame must have rankled deeply. Bernini had started his career as a painter and sculptor and, as with his renaissance predecessors, regarded this preparation as adequate training for an architect. Borromini, by the nature of his training as a mason, brought a high degree of specialised knowledge to his buildings and despised Bernini's technical failings.

This proficiency in his art, led him to make revolutionary innovations and to abandon the classical conventions of structure still held to by Bernini and to replace them by a system of geometric units.

Borromini's great opportunity came in 1633, with the commission for the church of S. Carlo alle Quattro Fontane (1638–46). The site is very small, irregular and constricted yet within its perimeter he devised an original spatial composition including a small cloister. S. Carlo is built up of three distinct units, undulating walls in the lower part, an intermediary zone and then an oval honeycombed dome (Fig. 5). The very plastic treatment of the walls with their columns accentuates the rhythmic undulation, but the movement is steadied by the firm ring of the oval dome, which gives the impression of greater height by reduction in size of its coffering towards the lantern. In spite of the disparity of the elements, the whole merges into a rich harmony. This diversity within a unifying theme is elaborated in the façade, the convex/concave rhythm referring back to the interior.

His later works were either left unfinished or were adaptations of buildings begun by other architects. They became increasingly unorthodox. In the Palazzo Falconieri (Fig. 7), for example, he made the top floor with its open loggia become the most dominant feature, reversing the normal process of gradation. Inside he executed a series of twelve ceilings decorated with an elaborate and unusual floral ornament. The last years saw a move towards an almost oppressively monumental and austere style. His neurotic character eventually drove him to suicide.

In the 1650s he had designed the *gran salone* and gallery of the Palazzo Pamphili in the Piazza Navona, containing some of the most original of his door surrounds. The frescoes in this gallery were contributed by Pietro da Cortona, the final figure of the Roman trio and nearly as versatile a genius as Bernini. His ceiling in the Barberini Palace (Fig. 8) has a wealth of simulated stucco decoration partly concealing the illusionistic framework. It creates a dual illusion of space behind the framework and in front of it, with a mass of figures appearing to hover on the simulated stucco work within the room itself. Strong lighting effects and foreshortening are used to increase the sensation of mass and movement leading through to the glowing light around the central figure of Divine Providence. The giant bees flying in formation are the heraldic emblems of the Barberini family. The variety of shape, illusion and colour with the great swirl of its inhabitants must make the most impressive of baroque ceilings.

In the 1640s, Cortona was occupied with a series of frescoes in the Grand Duke's suite of rooms at the Palazzo Pitti in Florence. These were named after Jupiter, Venus, Mars, Apollo and Saturn and have a marvellous, decorative richness (Fig. 4). A festive spirit pervades the whole cycle with the complete gamut of baroque stucco decoration piled layer on layer in the frames of the scenes. Yet this is not an illusionistic scheme. The decoration is, in fact, laid over the architecture, not merged with it, and the gilt or white stucco frames starkly define the pictorial space. It was the classicising balance between dignified grandeur and exuberant ornament that was to become the established style for aristocratic interiors

Fig. 6 ***Façade of Sta. Susanna,*** *Rome, by Carlo Maderno (1556–1629), 1603.*
The façade has the same two-storied arrangement and giant scrolls which conceal the roof line of the side aisles as the mannerist façade of Il Gesù *by Vignola. The logical arrangement of the pilasters and columns is completely new, however, pointing to one of the main differences between Mannerism and the Baroque.*

Fig. 7 ***Façade of the Palazzo Falconieri,*** *Rome, by Francesco Borromini (1599–1680)* c.*1640. Throughout his work Borromini flouted tradition. Here, he reversed the normal architectural progression by making the top storey into an open loggia, which consequently becomes the most dominant feature.*

4

Scala

5

Scala

6

Hamlyn Group

7

Mansell Collection

and to influence more than anything else the formulation of the *style Louis XIV*.

With the death of Borromini, Bernini and Cortona, the supremacy of Rome declined. The Papacy was no longer in a financial or political position to act as supreme patron of the arts, a role now increasingly challenged by France.

In Italy, the north now became a more interesting centre of activity. In Piedmont, the Royal House of Savoy was emerging as a dominant power and this found expression in an expansion of building activity in Turin in the latter part of the seventeenth century. Guarino Guarini (1624–83) was a philosopher and mathematician and his architecture shows a love for abstract geometry in an amazing complexity of forms, for example in the incredible conical dome of his Capella della SS. Sindone (1667–90). His admiration for the achievements of Borromini is obvious and in his Palazzo Carignano (1679) with its oval saloon and undulating façade, he expands the forms of San Carlo alle Quattro Fontane into palatial terms.

With the succession to the throne of Savoy of Victor Amadeus II, a need was felt by the Crown to surround itself with magnificent architecture in

Fig. 8 ***Ceiling of the Palazzo Barberini,** Rome, by Pietro da Cortona (1596–1669), 1633–39. This staggering piece of decoration illustrates the full meaning of the Baroque. It is so carefully and logically planned that it is impossible to tell what is real and what painted as hosts of mythological figures seated on clouds and flying freely across the decorated space present the figure of Divine Providence in the centre of the heavens, bathed in a golden light. The giant bees flying in formation are the emblem of the Barberini family.*

Scala

rivalry to the glories of Versailles. The man appointed as 'First Architect to the King' was Filippo Juvarra (1678–1736). Two of his great royal works were the front of the Palazzo Madama (1718–21) and the hunting lodge, or rather palace of Stupinigi (1719 onwards). The Palazzo Madama façade is a far more successful version of J. H. Mansart's Versailles garden approach, bringing a proper emphasis to the dominance of the first floor, as established by Bernini at the Palazzo Chigi-Odescalchi. The façade forms the outer wall of a magnificent staircase hall, a brilliant paraphrase of Versailles and its Galerie des Glaces, in the relation of its arcaded inner wall to the round-headed windows.

Stupinigi (Fig. 2) is Juvarra's masterpiece in its amazing scale and plan. The splendid two-storied hall forms the centre of the composition with wings radiating on either side containing exquisitely decorated reception and living rooms. Here is a grand fulfilment of Bernini's Louvre projects.

Juvarra's style can be taken as the culmination of the Baroque in Italy. He was not so much an innovator as the creator of a brilliant synthesis of the grand idioms developed during the course of the seventeenth century. The universality of the Baroque with the intimate relationship of all the arts creating the entire building, was to be broken up. The new age, after the transition of the Rococo, brought a more restrained and isolationist approach to both interior and exterior. JG

FURTHER READING

The Penguin Dictionary of Architecture by John Fleming, Hugh Honour and Nikolaus Pevsner, Baltimore, 1966.

Bernini by Howard Hibbard, London, 1965.

Art and Architecture in Italy, 1600–1750 by Rudolf Wittkower, London, revised edition, 1965.

Italian Villas and Palaces by Georgina Masson, London, 1959.

ITALIAN BAROQUE PALACES AND CHURCHES

The following Italian baroque palaces and churches may be visited. Visitors should bear in mind that Italian palaces and churches often close for several hours in the middle of the day.

PALACES

Palazzo Barberini, Rome. Now the National Gallery in Rome.

Palazzo Farnese, Rome. The Gallery is open to the public only on Sundays.

Royal Palace, Caserta (Palazzo Reale), near Naples. Open weekdays and Sundays.

Palazzo Pitti, Florence. The part in which the Cortona frescoes are situated is now the Galleria Palatina and houses some of the most magnificent high renaissance paintings including famous works by Titian and Raphael. Open weekdays and Sundays. Closed on Tuesdays.

Palazzo Madama, Turin. Open weekdays and Sundays.

Palazzina della Caccia, Stupinigi, Piedmont. Closed Mondays and Fridays, Jan. 1st and Nov. 1st, Easter and Christmas Days.

CHURCHES

St. Peter's, Rome. Open every day until half an hour before the evening service.

S. Carlo alle Quattro Fontane, Rome. All week and all day Sunday. The Church is generally locked but during opening hours one applies to the monastery by ringing the bell next door to the church.

Sa. Maria della Vittoria, Rome. Open weekdays and Sundays.

Il Gesù, Rome. Open weekdays and Sundays.

Capella SS. Sindone, Turin. The chapel is in St. John's Cathedral (Duomo S. Giovanni) which is open every day.

Furniture for Display

William Collier

Steve Fletcher

Fig. 1 **Wall candle bracket,** *north Italian, seventeenth century. Pine, carved and painted, height 58 ins., width 26 ins.*
This magnificent candleholder was originally one of twenty-four of exceptional size and beauty. They would have been made for one of the great families of northern Italy, and it is possible that the horseman in the central plaque has some connection with the house of which the coat of arms is displayed.
(Dark and Rendlesham, London.)

Stimulated by the excesses of baroque art, and seeking the appearance of splendour rather than any real domestic comfort, furniture in seventeenth-century Italy became richly theatrical and magnificently grotesque.

For early signs of the baroque style in Italy we must look to the fine arts. In Gianlorenzo Bernini's early sculptures, for example, around 1620, can be found the combined tension and exuberance of the Baroque, expressive of the mood of the time in Rome. The news of the victory by the Imperial Catholic army in Bohemia over the Protestants at the Battle of the White Mountain, the opening battle of the Thirty Years' War, was received with great rejoicing by the Pope and cardinals, for one of whom Bernini erected his great statue of Neptune and Triton (Fig. 2, page 1846). Something of the same confident assertiveness animated the Venetians in their long struggle against the infidel Turk in Crete and the Morea; they too gave expression to this spirit in their art.

A sketch for a table decoration carried out in sugar

Contemporary engravings of feasts and pageants show how a style originating with the fine arts came to be formulated in terms also of decoration and furniture. The celebrated sculptured group at Livorno of *Ferdinand I and Moorish captives*, for example, was reproduced in miniature as a table decoration for a feast given by the great collector of the mid-seventeenth century, Cardinal Leopoldo de' Medici. Such ceremonial festivities, one of the few expressions of political activity in Italian oligarchies and principalities, attained great importance in Rome, Venice and Florence for the welcome of a distinguished visitor, to celebrate a marriage alliance or simply to emphasise the power and wealth of the state. It was a sculptor, Antonio Corradini who, in the early eighteenth century, designed the new Bucentaur state barge in which the doge annually performed the symbolical wedding of Venice with the sea. Bernini himself was called upon to design a throne for Queen Christina of Sweden when she dined in state with Pope Alexander VII and he was not above providing a sketch for a table decoration to be carried out in sugar.

Although the wealth of Italy declined in the seventeenth century, a small number of families in the Pope's dominions and in the oligarchic republics of Genoa and Venice accumulated and kept great riches. The families of papal nephews and the commoners who bought their way into the Venetian patriciate during the wars with Turkey rivalled the richest of the older nobility in the splendour of their new palaces, each with its suite of grand reception rooms devoted to display. It was for such palaces in Rome that furniture was first designed in a style which by its ostentation matched the social and political ambitions of its owners. Although not usually made at the same time as the rooms as part of a single decorative scheme, the chairs, cabinets, looking-glasses and console tables had to be of suitable design to be ranged against walls hung with Genoese velvets, Luccan silk, damask or gilt leather (Figs. 10 and 11). Some of the massiveness and richness of this furniture, which obtrudes when it is displayed out of context, can be seen as appropriate in these high rooms under the painted ceilings of Pietro da Cortona and his followers.

On the floors above, in smaller rooms where the owners lived much of their daily lives, furniture continued to be of the simpler type common throughout palaces in the sixteenth century. Little of it has survived, since it was constantly used and not highly valued, but we know from the few examples that remain and from paintings that it was stained rather than gilt and the better pieces were of walnut. Fig. 8 shows one of the more

Fig. 2 **Alcove of the nuptial chamber at La Rocca,** *Italian, seventeenth century.*
This astonishing room is a typical, if somewhat exaggerated, example of the excesses of the Baroque. The bed, with its gilt testiera, *or canopy, and appliquéed velvet hangings, would seem over-ornate in most other surroundings, but here it balances the magnificence of the alcove for which it was designed; indeed, a lesser piece of furniture would be entirely dwarfed in this room.*
(La Rocca, Soragna, Italy.)

Fig. 3 **Armchair,** *Italian, seventeenth century. Carved walnut re-covered with velvet, height 48 ins., width 34 ins. Although less ostentatious than its gilt counterparts, this armchair with its elaborate carving was a common type in moderately wealthy houses.*
(Victoria and Albert Museum, London.)

Fig. 4 **Table from the Sale delle Donne Forti,** *Italian, seventeenth century. Gilt and carved wood, the top covered with red velvet. The gilt supports of this table are of a similar shape and ornamentation to those of contemporary chairs, cabinets, beds and even candlestands.*
(La Rocca, Soragna.)

elaborate chairs of this class decorated with baroque carvings within the traditional outlines but with few concessions to comfort.

On the grander, more typically baroque, furniture the bold sculptural carving goes beyond this boundary of straight lines and takes over the main forms. Much of it is essentially sculptors' furniture, introducing great leafy scrolls, swags and garlands of flowers, animal legs and feet, *putti* and small-scale human figures. In many parts of Italy, one even finds sculptors at work on these compositions: at Genoa, Anton Maria Maragliano (1664–1739) and the Parodi father and son, Giacomo Filippo (1630–1702) and Domenico (1668–1740), produced gilt-wood candlestands and table supports; at Venice perhaps the finest Italian sculptor of his age, Andrea Brustolon (1662–1732), created suites of superbly carved chairs and tables for the richest patrician families, including the Venier, Correr and Pisani.

Marble inlay was a particular Italian skill

Marble inlay of different colours is another aspect of the sculptural nature of Italian baroque furniture. Even before the late sixteenth century, when the Grand Duke of Tuscany established a state workshop for this art in Florence, the *Opificio delle Pietre Dure*, marble inlay was a particular Italian skill. The new factory specialised both in flat surfaces and in raised work, often representing fruit, and its products became sufficiently famous abroad to lead to a brisk export trade in inlaid, coloured marble table tops. Most of the exports went to France, where wooden table frames were provided. A cheaper version of this form of inlay was later made from the powdered selenite composition known as *scagliola*. Both the *pietre dure* and *scagliola* table tops made excellent, colourful pieces of display furniture in the reception rooms of palaces (Fig. 6).

A combination of inlay and relief work can often be found on the highly decorative cabinets of this period. Ebony, or wood stained to simulate ebony, provided the background, acting as a foil to bring out the colour and intricacy of the panels and gilt mounts. Nominally for storage of documents and small objects of value, the finest cabinets were in fact intended more for decoration than for use. Their shape lent itself as much to architectural as to sculptural treatment, as can be seen in Fig. 5, and one at least is known to have been designed by the architect Carlo Fontana.

As compared with the rather similar cabinets of south Germany and the Netherlands, the Italian cabinet, or *stipo*, of the seventeenth century (Fig. 11) is more varied in form and less box-like, reflecting the emphasis of baroque architecture in central and northern Italy on interesting outlines, to which the surface decoration is subordinate. An architectural treatment for the cabinet itself made a more telling effect in conjunction with the sculptural treatment of the supports, on which the figures appear to be carrying a miniature building. Less ambitious examples, such as those made for church vestries, can still be seen all over Italy and some have found their way to this country. A pair with painted glass panels which Sir Thomas Isham brought back from Naples in 1678 is still at Lamport Hall in Northamptonshire.

Painting of furniture increasingly used as a disguise for cheaper wood

Copper was also used for painted panels. As the seventeenth century advanced and the Italian states found themselves poorer as the result of wars, misgovernment and conspicuous but unproductive expenditure, the painting of furniture was increasingly resorted to as a disguise for cheaper wood. A coating of size on pine or fir, with fine gauze spread across cracks in the surfaces, provided the basis for a coat of background paint to which were added designs in the form of arabesques, flowers or small scenes. The paintwork was protected by final coverings of lacquer which by the eighteenth century took the improved form of the French invention known as '*Vernis Martin*'. Gilding in many cases continued to be used for the main mouldings. By the late seventeenth century, Chinese designs were being imitated in Venice but the main history of Italian *Chinoiserie* belongs to the subsequent rococo style of the next century.

5

Museum Photo

Fig. 5 ***Miniature double-doored cupboard*** *by Carlo Maruti, Sicilian, seventeenth century. Wood, overlaid with amber, height 16¾ ins., width 12⅜ ins. This exquisite replica of a large Italian cupboard was probably intended less as a useful storage space than as an object of beauty in its own right. The panels of amber are as carefully set as fine inlaid work of the period, and the decorative carving is executed with extraordinary intricacy. Even the proportions of the piece have sacrificed nothing to its small size; architectural details such as the pilasters along the front and mouldings around the panels are faithful to cabinet-work of the time.*
(Victoria and Albert Museum.)

Fig. 6 ***Pietre dure table,*** *Italian, seventeenth century. Carved wood with inlaid marble, width 44 ins.*
Inlaid marble was a popular form of table decoration.
(Sotheby and Co., London.)

A. C. Cooper

Fig. 8 **Chair,** *Italian, seventeenth century. Carved walnut with inlaid oval of lighter wood, height 42 ins., width 17¾ ins., depth 12¾ ins.*
This type of chair was used in the smaller rooms of large palaces. Stained rather than gilded, they were elaborately carved and very uncomfortable.
(Wallace Collection, London. By kind permission of the Trustees.)

Raymond Fortt

Fig. 7 ***Candlestand in the form of a putto,*** *one of a pair, Florentine, c.1685. Carved wood with original gilding, height 49 ins.*
Although candles do not, in fact, need a great deal of support, candlestands of the period, called torciere, *were boldly carved.* Putti, *often with wings as in this case, were a favourite motif.*
(Spink and Son, Ltd., London.)

With the gradual spread of foreign styles, Italian baroque furniture lost some of its direct inspiration from the native fine arts of sculpture, architecture and painting and gained in the process a variety which makes the transitional stages between Baroque and Rococo a fascinating field of enquiry. The influence of French Louis XIV furniture can be detected in curved stretchers, panel decoration in gilt relief and panelled legs with husk pendants. French patterns were copied on both inlaid and painted furniture from the engravings of Jean and Daniel Marot, Jean le Pautre and the brothers Bérain. But until at least the productions of the second quarter of the eighteenth century, the distinctive character of Italian furniture is still very readily apparent if one examines its different forms.

The gilt supports for tables, chairs and cabinets exhibit strong similarities to each other, as can be seen by comparing those illustrated. Even when support was only needed for candles, the designs, often for church altars, were equally boldly carved with figure sculpture and strong mouldings (Fig. 8). Wall candle brackets were almost as elaborate on a smaller scale (Fig. 1). Similar relief carving to go against walls was applied to the wooden bedhead, or *testiera*, while a rather lighter carved framework went around the bed canopy. The same deep-coloured velvets were used for seat covers as for canopy hangings, the latter ornamented by appliqué designs, as on the magnificent bed in Fig. 2. Similarly, the embroidered material with which the bedhead was covered, especially in Piedmont, echoed the painted designs on wood furniture.

Wardrobes, bureaux and chests of drawers, all fairly utilitarian pieces of furniture which might be expected to differ more widely according to particular needs, in fact share characteristics which were present in Italian architecture: their tops are marked by cornices, curving wherever possible, and their angles by pilasters. More distinctively baroque are the serpentine fronts which appear on furniture towards the end of the seventeenth century but which can be found in Italian architecture as early as Borromini's Convento dei Filippini, Rome, of 1637.

The most ingenious application of baroque motifs is to be found in mirrors with glass frames which convey as much colour and flamboyance as the carved furniture of the period, despite the fact that the mirrors continue, as in the sixteenth century, to be mostly rectangles or octagons. Their geometrical severity is reduced by the device of two frames. The inner one follows the mirror's outline but usually employs some coloured glass and, in the eighteenth century, incised flowing patterns; the outer, which may be only a top cresting, spreads into the pierced curving lines of branches and foliage (Fig. 10). The extraordinary skill with which the glass-workers of Murano, Venice and Altare constructed these mirrors and frames produced an equally extraordinary demand. Mirrors did not really fit baroque design because, being flat and in themselves colourless, they were neither sculptural, pictorial nor architectural; yet owing to the *tour de force* of Italian technique and design, they became immensely popular. Very few glass mirrors were used in the sixteenth century but by 1644 John Evelyn was recording a number of large ones in the

8

Museum Photo

9

Museum Photo

10

Scala

Fig. 9 ***State chair,*** *one of a set of eight, probably Venetian, first half of the eighteenth century. Carved and gilt pine, upholstered with velvet brocade in green and crimson on a cream ground. Height 61 ins., width 36 ins., depth 45 ins. (Wallace Collection.)*

Fig. 10 ***View of the nuptial chamber at La Rocca*** *(see also Fig. 2), showing typical tables and armchairs, a carved wood mirror on the left, and a glass framed mirror on the right. (La Rocca, Soragna.)*

Fig. 11 ***View of the throne room at La Rocca,*** *showing the throne and a typical cabinet of the period with gilt sculptural supports. (La Rocca, Soragna.)*

11

Scala

Villa Borghese at Rome.

It was largely the lavish use of mirrors in Italian palaces that led to the many mirror rooms in western Europe, notably the Galerie des Glaces at Versailles. And one is reminded of the contribution which Italian baroque furniture has made to that of other countries, not least to England, where the furniture of William Kent derives directly from Roman examples.

FURTHER READING

Mobili intarsiati del sei e settecento in Italia by Edi Baccheschi, Milan, 1964.

Il mobile Italiano dal XV al XIX secolo by Piero Pinto, Novara, 1962.

The practical book of Italian, Spanish and Portuguese furniture by H. D. Eberlein and R. W. Ramsdell, Philadelphia, 1927.

A History of Italian furniture from the 14th to the early 19th centuries, 2 Vols, by William M. Odom, New York, 1918–19.

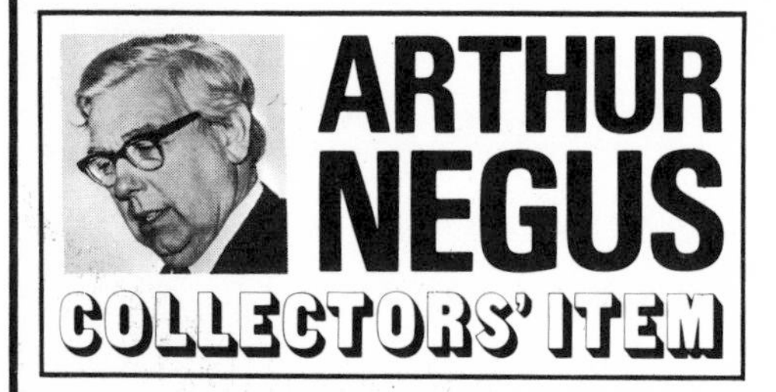

CAMEO JEWELLERY

Delicately carved in *bas-relief* with portraits or scenes that depend on the idealised grace of classical art, cameos, though unpretentious, are perhaps one of the most appealing forms of jewellery. They are an ancient art, first devised thousands of years ago by the Romans and Egyptians and imitated by succeeding generations ever since.
The material selected for this type of work usually has stratified layers of colour and the figure is cut in relief in one layer while another layer, of contrasting colour, serves as the background.
The reverse process, in which the design is incised into the ground, is called *intaglio* and this, too, was a popular form of decoration.
The appeal of finely-cut cameos can easily be understood and at various periods in history they have come into the forefront of fashion. The Renaissance produced many beautiful examples and the passion for the 'Antique' in the latter part of the eighteenth century and the early nineteenth century extended to this classical form of jewellery. But it was in the Victorian age, when all kinds of jewellery were highly fashionable, that they reached the peak of their popularity. Brooches, pendants, necklaces, ear-rings, and even chatelaines, were decorated with cameos.
Shell cameos came into their own during this Victorian revival of the art. In these, designs were cut from conch shells with a figure in white contrasted by a ground of pink, tan or maroon. Obviously the thin layer of a shell called for very delicate cutting and one can only marvel at the quality of the craftsmanship, particularly in the early examples.
Finer cameos were cut in sardonyx – red and white – black and white onyx, and agates, which could be a variety of colours. Opals, ivory and precious stones – emeralds, for example – were cut with cameos too, but these, because of their prohibitive cost, were much less common.
The major centres for cameo cutting during the nineteenth century were in Italy, where they were carving shells as early as in the 1820s, and in Germany, although production there was not so prolific. England supplied a great number of the shells to Europe but native English cutters were late in establishing themselves.

Collecting Hints

The best examples are those of an early date. The cutting is fine and importance is placed on the effects of light and shade and on the graceful contour. After 1860 the quality tended to deteriorate and by the 1870s the vogue was almost at an end.
In the late 1880s there was an attempt at revival and many small cameos found today such as rings, buttons and ear-rings, are from this period. They tend not to be as fine as the earlier ones but good quality craftsmanship from this date can occasionally be found. The best guide is a good eye, and only with practice can one learn to distinguish the delicacy of a good cameo from the coarser quality of so many of the later ones. Some shell cameo figures were mounted on agate and the prospective buyer should guard against mistaking this type for a completely agate cameo.
It is difficult to date a cameo stylistically since they all imitate classical art as closely as possible but, again, a trained eye can detect traces of fashionable form which tend to find their way into any imitative art.
Pinchbeck was also used, as was cut steel, and cameos are also found unmounted.

Subjects

The most popular subject was the portrait bust, cut in profile, with classical detail such as the hair style and the flowing drapery loosely arranged on the shoulders. Other less common subjects include chariot racing, neo-classical nymphs in a variety of pastoral settings, mythological scenes and family coats of arms.

Names To Look For

Cameos are sometimes signed with carved letters (often in Greek) on the front or back of the piece. Early in the nineteenth century, makers included Pichler, Pistucci, Morelli, Berini and Odelli. Later in the century, Isler and Saulini were among the finer craftsmen.

Prices

Prices vary enormously. Cheapest are unmounted cameos which can be purchased for less than £8, unless they are very fine. Gold mounted shell cameos fetch £15–£100 depending on size, quality and the amount of carving. Good stone cameos set in gold frames fetch £60–£300.
Frames can add enormously to the price. Set with gems such as rubies and diamonds, there is no limit to the top price.

Bottom left: Left to right: ***Phoebus riding his Chariot*** *signed by Saulini, shell. £75.* ***Angel*** *in a decorative gold frame, late Victorian, shell. £57 10s (£57·50).* ***Aurora,*** *shell. £95.*

Bottom right: Top left: ***Portrait head,*** *onyx, mounted in gold and pearls. £195.*
Top right: ***Portrait of Jane Austen,*** *shell, £60.* Centre: ***Winged head, possibly Mercury,*** *agate, £97 10s (£97·50).* Bottom left: ***Vulcan,*** *shell, £80.* Bottom right: ***Bacchante,*** *shell, £60.*

Opposite: ***Portrait head,*** *sardonyx, mounted in gold set with pearls, £275.*
(All cameos from Cameo Corner, London, W.C.1.)

Cameo Corner: A. C. Cooper

Cameo Corner: A. C. Cooper

THEATRE AND COS

Until almost the middle of the seventeenth century, Italian opera and ballet were developed chiefly for the pleasure of princes and occasional performances at their private courts. The first move towards public performances on any scale was initiated by Venice, where the success of the Teatro San Cassiano, opened in 1637, prompted the opening of four other opera houses within four years. Spectacular scenery and costumes were supplemented by highly elaborate stage machinery, all of which had a revolutionary influence on the development of stage design throughout Europe.

Fig. 1 ***Setting for the ballet*** Il Carnevale Languente, *performed for the Court of Savoy in Turin, 1647. Water-colour from the manuscript of the ballet. (Professor Attilio Bigo Collection.)*

Fig. 2 ***Costume for the ballet*** Il Carnevale Languente *(see Fig. 1). Water-colour. The Marquis of San Damiano is seen as Choleric Fiery Humour, one of the elements. (Professor Attilio Bigo Collection.)*

B. Gascoigne, 'World Theatre'

DESIGNS
UMES

B. Gascoigne, 'World Theatre'

17th century Italian Theatrical Design

3

Scala

4

B. Gascoigne, 'World Theatre'

5

Scala

Fig. 3 ***Setting for the ballet*** Lisimaco, *performed in the Teatro Ducale in Turin, 1681. Water-colour. (Biblioteca Nazionale, Turin.)*

Fig. 4 ***Interior of the Teatro Ducale at Turin,*** *later known as the Teatro Regio. The scene is set for a performance of the ballet* Lisimaco *given in Turin in 1681. Water-colour from the manuscript. (Biblioteca Nazionale.)*

Fig. 5 ***Teatro Olimpico, detail of the auditorium,*** *designed by Andrea Palladio (1618–80) for the Accademia Olimpica in Vicenza, begun in 1680, first used in 1685.*
It was designed on the principles of the Roman architect Vitruvius to look like an ancient open-air theatre, and the ceiling painted with sky and clouds heightens this illusion. Palladio died the same year that it was begun, but his design had a strong influence on the work of his English follower, Inigo Jones.

Fig. 6 ***Courtyard of a castle*** *by Ferdinando Galli-Bibiena (1657–1743). Engraving.*
First of the renowned family of stage-designers, the Bibienas, Ferdinando is thought to have developed the dramatic use of perspective called scena per angolo, *employed throughout the eighteenth century.*
(Victoria and Albert Museum, London.)

Fig. 7 ***Costumes used at the Festival of Rome,*** *25 February, 1634, possibly by Andrea Sacchi, Italian, seventeenth century. Engraving. (Victoria and Albert Museum.)*

Fig. 8 ***Setting designed by Giacomo Torelli,*** *engraving by Israel Silvestre (1621–91), 1654. Torelli was one of the greatest of Italian stage designers, whose changeable scenery and mechanical devices astounded and influenced all Europe.*

6

Museum Photo

7

Museum Photo

8

Bulloz

Fig. 9 ***Palazzo della Fama*** *designed by Giulio Parigi, 1608. Etching by Remigio Cantagallina in the same year.*
Giulio Parigi was a Florentine stage designer whose sets had a profound influence on seventeenth-century theatres throughout Europe. He studied under Buontalenti, a pre-eminent designer of the late sixteenth century, and became Buontalenti's successor as chief stage designer to the Medici family. His designs, along with those of his son Alfonso, were published as etchings which were sent to many different countries. They had a great influence on Inigo Jones, who had also spent three years in Italy studying, among other things, the sets of Parigi, and who returned at least once in later life to Florence. He was also indebted to Parigi for his costume designs and for his general approach to the problems of the theatre.
(Victoria and Albert Museum.)

9

10

Museum Photo

11

Bulloz

Fig. 10 ***Act IV scene 14 from*** Il Pomo d'Oro, *designed by Lodovico Burnacini, performed in Vienna, 1668. The engraving from a series depicting the principal scenes, by Mattha'us Küsel.*
Viennese court operas of the seventeenth century rivalled even those of Italy for sheer magnificence. Lodovico Burnacini's father Giovanni was imported from Venice to design sets by the Holy Roman Emperor himself; but it was the son who created the most lavish productions. Il Pomo d'Oro *had twenty-two completely different changes of scenery, each of which had more detail and more interest than those of any earlier designer. Burnacini was also an enthusiastic user of complicated stage machinery for the production of special effects.*
(Victoria and Albert Museum.)

Fig. 11 ***Setting designed by Giacomo Torelli,*** *engraving by Israel Silvestre, mid-seventeenth century.*

1

Arms and Armour

Vesey Norman

Scala

16th and 17th century
Italian Armour

Fig. 1 (previous page) ***Open-faced helmet and round shield*** *by Gasparo Mola, c.1609. Steel overlaid with silver-gilt.*
These highly decorated but totally impractical pieces were made for Cosimo II, Grand Duke of Tuscany.
(Museo Bargello, Florence.)

Fig. 2 ***Armour of Louis XIV*** *possibly by Giovan Battista da Garbagno of Brescia, mid-seventeenth century. Presented by the Republic of Venice to the King in 1668.*
(Musée de l'Armée, Paris.)

2

Ciné son Pichonnier

3

Foto Bertoni

Fig. 3 ***Sword hilt*** *by Pietro Ancini, signed and dated 1641. Chiselled steel.*
This light dress sword bears the arms of the Medici family.
(Museo Bargello.)

Used not only for protection, but also as a symbol of wealth and military prowess, armour in seventeenth-century Italy ranged from the strictly functional to the magnificently sumptuous.

All over Europe in the seventeenth century, field armours were short-waisted with square, clumsy-looking shoulder-defences (pauldrons), and with a long series of narrow, horizontal strips (lames) protecting the lower part of the trunk and the legs to below the knees. The surface was broken up by numerous laminations and brass-headed rivets. Even the Italian flair for design could do little to mitigate their ungainly lines. Portraits by such painters as Anthony van Dyck and Justus Sustermans, both of whom worked in Italy, show even the most illustrious commanders wearing plain armour in this fashion, either blued or painted black.

To flutter the hearts of the loveliest and haughtiest ladies

Some portraits of this period still show armour etched with bands of decoration in the style carried over from the previous century, while some important armours survive which are etched and gilt all over with reticulated designs enclosing a variety of devices. The scrolls forming the network often include knots, in some cases of the type used by the ducal family of Savoy as one of its badges. The devices in the interspaces also include those used by the house of Savoy. Van Dyck's portrait of Emanuele Filiberto, third son of Carlo Emanuele I of Savoy, painted in 1624, shows him in armour decorated exactly in this way (Fig. 10). An armour at Naples decorated in a somewhat similar manner, without knots, but with the fleur-de-lis of Farnese in the interspaces, probably belonged to one of the young sons of Ranuccio I, Duke of Parma.

The technique of etching used on these armours is that adopted earlier from Germany with the decoration in slight relief and the background covered with small raised dots. In a cheaper form of decoration the design was only outlined by etching, engraving or incising, and the surface of the motifs fire-gilt against a russet or blued ground. Reticulated patterns were produced in this technique but in many cases the surface was simply powdered with devices and monograms at regular intervals.

As well as these three-quarter suits, called cuirassier armours in England (Figs. 8 and 9), there were armours for dismounted service; these had shorter thigh defences (tassets), sometimes made by temporarily removing the knee-defences and the plates immediately above them from the cuirassier armour. An open helmet was usually worn, sometimes of a type with a peak over the eyes and a deep laminated neck-guard derived from a Turkish helmet. Towards the middle of the century the divided tassets were sometimes replaced by a heavy skirt of three to six lames. The pauldrons were extended to cover the upper arms, and the defences

4

J. Freeman

5

A. C. Cooper

for the lower arms were abandoned.

During the first part of the century, armours for the very wealthy were still made in sets which were decorated to match. These usually consisted of a field armour for mounted combat, sometimes with reinforces (reinforcements) for the tilt, an infantry commander's armour and, finally, an armour for the tournament on foot, usually with a round shield (target).

Armour had purposes other than simply to defend its wearer. A magnificent harness gleaming with gold and highly polished steel, set off with gaily coloured plumes and textiles, demonstrated the

6

7

Fig. 4 ***Light dress sword hilt*** *in the style of Carlo Bottarello of Brescia, late seventeenth century. Chiselled steel. (Wallace Collection, London. By permission of the Trustees.)*

Fig. 5 ***Cup-hilted sword and left-hand dagger in the Spanish style*** *by Antonio Cilenta, Naples, c.1650. Pierced and chiselled steel. (Victoria and Albert Museum.)*

Fig. 6 ***Cavalry sword hilt,*** *probably North Italian, c.1650. Chiselled steel. (Wallace Collection.)*

Fig. 7 ***Cavalry sword hilt,*** *Italian, c.1600. Gold decoration. This magnificently decorated sword belonged to Count Pio Capodilista. On the blade are his initials and armorial device. (Wallace Collection.)*

wealth and importance of its owner. It gave him an air of military glamour sufficient to stir the courage of his most hesitant follower and, no doubt, to flutter the hearts of the loveliest and haughtiest ladies. By this time the tournament had become less of a contest and more of a display of horsemanship. Running at a ring hung over the lists, or at a dummy Turk, gradually replaced tilting against a live opponent. The tournament proper gave way to the 'carousel', an elaborate equestrian ballet for which real armour was no longer needed.

Specially decorated armours were made for these impressive displays, as well as for important ceremonial occasions at Court. For example, an open helmet and a target in the Museo Bargello, Florence (Fig. 1), made about 1609 for Cosimo II, Grand Duke of Tuscany, are of blued steel but are covered in a delicate and very elaborate network of grotesques, scrolls, and strap-work in silver-gilt. They would be quite impractical as armour but very suitable to display the taste and wealth of the owner. The maker of these pieces was the goldsmith Gasparo Mola, who was employed by the grand dukes of Tuscany from 1609, and later worked at the papal mint in Rome until his death in 1640.

Towards the end of the century, when armour was almost entirely obsolete except for the cuirass, applied decoration was still sometimes used. A horse's head defence (shaffron) and a cuirass in the Armeria Reale, Turin, are decorated with an elaborate overlay of gilt-copper trophies of arms, laurel and acanthus foliage, all chased in relief against a russeted steel ground.

Armour was a symbol of military prowess

Commanders were usually painted in armour, or with pieces of it beside them, long after it was actually given up in the field, because of its importance as a symbol of military prowess. A fine armour was therefore a very suitable present with which to honour a prince. Probably the last complete armour made was presented by the Republic of Venice in 1668 to Louis XIV, fresh from his victorious campaign in the Low Countries (Fig. 2). The engraving decorating it is signed by Francesco da Garbagno of Brescia and the armour was probably actually made by his brother Giovan Battista. The decoration on the armour consists of foliate ovals containing scenes of the King's victories based on a series of engravings by Van der Meulen.

Not a great deal is known about the making of sword blades in Italy, since many of the surviving blades with Italian signatures betray, by the spelling of the names, their German origin. Confusion is made greater by the fact that blades were signed both by the smith who forged them and by the craftsmen who finished them; in some cases, these might be many miles apart in different provinces.

Thus names and marks occur together in an endless variety of combinations. For instance, blades forged in Friuli might be finished and mounted in Milan. A blade in the Wallace Collection signed by a member of the Lambertenghi family of Milan also bears the mark of an unidentified but very prolific bladesmith working at Caino. There were numerous centres of production right across the north of Italy from Genoa in the west to Friuli in the east.

In Brescia, for instance, where in the early seventeenth century there were no less than two hundred workshops of sword cutlers and allied trades, blades were bought in the rough from the neighbouring towns of Caino and Navi, in Brescian territory, or from Gromo, in the territory of Bergamo. They first passed to the grinding shops situated in the suburbs of the city, and then to the polishers and gilders for the final finishing.

The hilts supplied to the haftmakers of Brescia were bought in the rough state from the villages of Gardone, Lumazzane and Inzione, and were polished, coloured and chiselled by specialist craftsmen in the city (Fig. 4), mainly working in the street running from the Porteghi della Spadaria to the Piazza Grande. Probably some of the hilts were exported unmounted, as gun parts certainly were. Some of the specialist chisellers made spurs as well as sword hilts, others probably also decorated the gun mounts for which the city was famous. This was certainly the case elsewhere. Petrus Ancinus, who signed a finely chiselled hilt in the Museo Bargello bearing the Medici arms and the date 1641 (Fig. 3) and another hilt in the Musée de

8

J. Freeman

9

Museum Photo

l'Armée, Paris, dated 1661, also signed the richly chiselled lock and trigger-guard of a gun in 1643. He is probably Pietro Ancini, the sculptor and painter of Reggio Emilia (1616–1702).

Naples and Sicily were at this time possessions of Spain, and Spanish fashions predominated there, including the long bladed, cup-hilted rapier with its matching left-hand dagger (*dago de mano izquierda*) (Fig. 5). The blued steel of the hilts is usually pierced with a lace-like design of spiral scrolls, sometimes including eagles or small wren-like birds, and sometimes human figures or grotesque masks. Although hilts signed by their makers are generally rare, curiously enough this type is the exception, and a number are signed by craftsmen working, not only as one would expect in Naples and Palermo, but also in Milan. The earliest illustration of a cup-hilt is in a portrait of Philip IV of Spain, painted about 1623–24. They remained in use in provincial Spain until the last quarter of the eighteenth century. A few exist with dates considerably earlier than 1623 but these are probably the results of 'over-restoration' by nineteenth-century dealers.

An enamelled gold swept hilt with matching left-hand dagger

Elsewhere in Italy, during the first half of the seventeenth century, the so-called 'swept hilt' appears to have been the most popular style, but it is rarely possible to point to a specifically Italian example. A hilt of blued steel in the castle of Skokloster in Sweden, is chiselled with fine foliate scrolls ending in dragon heads strongly reminiscent of the decoration on Brescian gun mounts. An enamelled gold swept hilt with matching left-hand dagger and belt mounts in the Musée de l'Armée, Paris, has been identified as one mentioned as his own work in the will of Gasparo Mola, who made the armour of Cosimo II mentioned above. The guards are enamelled in the *champlevé* technique with elaborate scrolls and the pommels with human figures standing under canopies in the style of the overmantel designer Etienne Delaune, who died in about 1583.

Unfortunately, the absence of a national portrait gallery in Italy and the neglect of the study of seventeenth-century portraiture there, together with the failure of any great ancestral armoury to survive, makes it exceptionally difficult to study the changes of fashion in sword hilts. So far, all that can be said is that many hilts exist in the shapes fashionable in northern Europe, and particularly in France, during the second half of the seventeenth century. They are of pierced and chiselled blued steel, some rather in the style of Brescian gun mounts and others in the style of the cup-hilts discussed above. It is at present customary to call these Italian. In Italy, as in Spain, it remained fashionable to pass the forefinger over the front part of the cross-guard, to improve the hold on the sword, long after this was given up in France. This means that the small-sword, when it was introduced from northern Europe, was made with rather larger arms to the hilt than was customary in the north, so as to accommodate the forefinger between the cross and the protective shell in front of the hand.

10

Museum Photo

Fig. 8 (far left) ***Cuirassier armour**, Milanese, c.1600–10. This impressive armour was probably made for a prince of the House of Savoy, and would have been intended as much as a status symbol as a means of protection. (Wallace Collection.)*

Fig. 9 (left) ***Cuirassier armour**, probably Brescian, c.1640–50. Made for Count Annibale Capodilista, this armour of the three-quarter or cuirassier type is essentially a fighting armour. (Glasgow Art Gallery and Museum, Scott Collection.)*

Fig. 10 (above) ***Emanuele Filiberto, third son of Carlo Emanuele I of Savoy** by Sir Anthony Van Dyck (1599–1641), 1624. (Dulwich College Picture Gallery, London.)*

CARE OF SWORDS AND ARMOUR

1. Arms and armour, by their very nature, are particularly liable to damage by rust. As far as possible they should be kept where they cannot be touched. If they have been handled they should always be wiped with a clean, dry cloth before they are put away. Rust can form very quickly on fingerprints and makes a permanent mark.
2. Blades and bright armour can be protected by a thin coating of a mixture of Three-in-one oil and vaseline which has the added advantage of discouraging the casual toucher.
3. Alternatively, the steel can be coated with a colourless lacquer but great care must be taken that this does not get accidently chipped, or worn off by regular dusting, allowing rust to form on the exposed surface.
4. A silicone impregnated cloth has recently been developed with which arms and armour can be rubbed to give them a temporary protective coat.
5. Beyond the removal of purely superficial dirt no action to clean either arms or armour should ever be taken without expert advice. A few minutes spent applying elbow-grease too enthusiastically can do irreparable damage.
6. On no account should patent rust-removers be used on either arms or armour since these give a dead leaden appearance to the surface of the metal.

MUSEUMS AND COLLECTIONS

The following list is by no means complete, but it gives an idea of some of the major armour collections throughout the world:

GREAT BRITAIN

Edinburgh:	Royal Scottish Museum
Glasgow:	Art Gallery and Museum
London:	H.M. Tower of London Victoria and Albert Museum Wallace Collection
York:	Castle Museum

ITALY

Brescia:	Museo Civico, Marzoli
Schloss Churburg (in the Italian Tyrol)	Armoury of Count Trapp
Florence:	Museo Nazionale (Bargello), Museo Stibbert
Mantua:	Sanctuaria della Madonna della Grazie
Naples:	Museo e Gallerie Nazionali di Capodimonte
Rome:	Odescalchi Collection Museo Nazionale di Castel Sant'Angelo
Turin:	Armeria Reale
Venice:	Palazzo Ducale

ELSEWHERE IN EUROPE

Austria:	Waffensammlung, Vienna
Denmark:	Tøjhusmuseet, Copenhagen
France:	Musée de l'Armée, Paris
Spain:	Real Armería, Madrid
Sweden:	Livrustkammaren, Stockholm

U.S.A.

Baltimore:	Walters Art Gallery
New York:	Metropolitan Museum of Art
Worcester:	John Woodman Higgins Armory, Mass.

BAXTER PRINTS

George Baxter (1804–67) set up as an engraver in Blackfriars Road, London, in 1827, and he published *Butterflies*, his first coloured print, in 1830. This print was so successful that Baxter determined to perfect a method by which he could 'render a picture in its natural and proper colours'. He combined the ancient woodblock method with the newer metal-plate system, using ground-down oil colours for the many different blocks needed.

In 1835 Baxter secured a patent for his invention, and in the following ten years he illustrated more than a hundred volumes with some of his most famous prints. *The Coronation of Queen Victoria 1838* and *The Opening of Queen Victoria's First Parliament* established his reputation as a major artist. In 1838 Baxter published his first separate print, *The Departure of Camden*, rapidly followed by a series for the London Missionary Society. Although best known for his religious and sentimental subjects, Baxter also produced smaller, cheaper prints of topical interest. His best work combines an astonishing brilliance of tone with immaculate linework and delicate shading. The main categories of Baxter prints comprise the following: Missionary prints, the Great Exhibition of 1851 series, Crimean War prints, Portraits of the Famous, Religious prints, Interiors, Flowers and Fruit and Exteriors.

Hints to Collectors

Prints from Baxter's workshops nearly always carry the legend 'Printed in Oil Colours by Geo Baxter Patentee', or 'Printed by G. Baxter, the Inventor and Patentee of Oil Colour Printing'. These are either incorporated in the picture itself or, less often, embossed on the mount. Most prints also carry the address from which Baxter worked at the time, and this enables the collector to date his acquisitions with some accuracy. From 1830 to 1835, he worked at 29 King Square, Goswell Road; from 1835 to 1843 at 3 Charterhouse Square, and from 1843 to 1860 at 11 Northampton Square.

Prices

Early Baxter prints, from the mid- to late 1830s, can fetch as much as £25 while later examples, which are easier to find, generally sell for something in the region of £5 or £10.

Phillips Son & Neale: A. C. Cooper

Phillips Son & Neale: A. C. Cooper

Phillips Son & Neale: A. C. Cooper

Above: *Winter scene, one of a series of four prints depicting the seasons, c.£20.*

Centre: *Three sentimental scenes, typical of the many produced by Baxter for his less sophisticated patrons. It was quite usual for them to be mounted together in this way.*

Top: *Queen Victoria, Prince Albert and some of the royal children. Baxter produced a number of prints depicting the royal family.*

Opposite: *'Summertime', one of the most popular of Baxter's range of sentimental scenes, c.£10.*

Phillips Son & Neale: A. C. Cooper

Seventeenth-Century Bronzes

Italian bronzes of the seventeenth century were baroque in every sense of the word; crude, vigorous and dramatic, they were produced by little-known artists, and greatly influenced by the revolutionary work of Bernini.

1

Museum Photo

2

Museum Photo

3

Museum Photo

Fig. 1 ***Neptune,*** *Italian, seventeenth century. Height 1 ft. 9½ ins. Bernini's influence can be recognized in this work, which is derived from Fig. 2. (Victoria and Albert Museum, London.)*

Fig. 2 ***Neptune and Triton*** *by Bernini (1598–1680), Rome, c.1622. Marble, height 6 ft. ½ in. (Victoria and Albert Museum.)*

Fig. 3 ***The Florentine Boar*** *by Antonio Susini (d.1624), Florentine, early seventeenth century. Height 6½ ins. This is one of innumerable casts from a Roman original. (Victoria and Albert Museum.)*

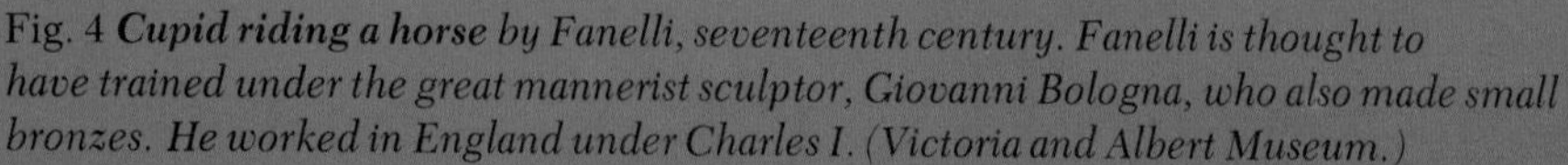

Fig. 4 ***Cupid riding a horse*** *by Fanelli, seventeenth century. Fanelli is thought to have trained under the great mannerist sculptor, Giovanni Bologna, who also made small bronzes. He worked in England under Charles I. (Victoria and Albert Museum.)*

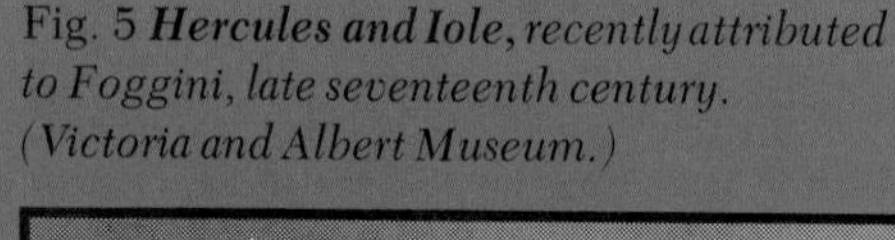

Fig. 5 ***Hercules and Iole,*** *recently attributed to Foggini, late seventeenth century. (Victoria and Albert Museum.)*

4

Museum Photo

5

Museum Photo

Unless otherwise stated the sculptures illustrating this article are of bronze.

Fig. 7 ***Saucer,*** *marked 'Vena A. G. 1726', Vezzi factory, 1726. Diameter 5½ ins., depth 1¼ ins. Painted with a mock heraldic design, this saucer was probably commissioned by an untitled citizen with social aspirations. (Museo Civico, Turin.)*

Fig. 8 ***Saucer,*** *Hewelcke factory, 1761–63. Diameter 5 ins. Founded by N. F. Hewelcke and his wife, who had emigrated to Venice from Dresden, this factory produced wares of inferior quality to those of Vezzi and Cozzi. The shapes are comparatively clumsy and the glazes and colours lack brilliance. (Victoria and Albert Museum.)*

Fig. 9 ***Teacup and saucer,*** *Cozzi factory, late eighteenth century. Polychrome decoration, height 3 ins., diameter of saucer 5 ins. These fine pieces are painted with a Venetian* capriccio. *(Victoria and Albert Museum.)*

Fig. 10 ***Teapot,*** *Vezzi factory, 1725. Raised and painted decoration. This charming example of Vezzi ware is derived from the popular octagonal shapes of eighteenth-century silverware. (Victoria and Albert Museum.)*

produce eight tureens and sets of cups and chocolate- and coffee-pots in white and gold.

Cozzi's enterprise flourished, and in 1767 he advertised in the *Giornale d'Italia* for more turners, modellers and painters, promising a good welcome and stipend. In order to protect the sale of Cozzi's porcelain, the Senate passed a law in 1771 increasing the duty on all imported porcelain. Cozzi was put in charge of the customs inspection. In 1781, the Senate made a further regulation forbidding the importation of Chinese, Japanese or other Asiatic porcelain, and forbidding the importation of any other kind of European porcelain for twenty years. As a further aid to the porcelain-makers, in 1785 the Senate forced the clay merchants to decrease their prices from one hundred *lire* per cart-load to eighty-six. This relieved Cozzi of a serious anxiety since the price of clay from Tretto upon which he depended had more than doubled over the previous twenty years.

In spite of all this, there were financial troubles. Cozzi had started out on very little capital and had had to borrow. At a later stage, money was raised by selling shares, but he got into litigation with his shareholders. The Board of Trade gave him two years to pay back the capital and interest. In 1784, he was able to dissolve the company and assume sole ownership of the factory.

The output of Cozzi's factory was enormous. Between 1784 and 1785, eighty-three people were employed in the production of eighty-four thousand saucers and cups and fifteen thousand decorative items, in addition to the articles made in maiolica. Cozzi's best customers were the State and the nobility, and they also included the Holy House of Loreto. Most of his work was on display and for sale in a shop in San Salvatore, where customers could buy anything from a coffee-cup to a figure or a clock-case. In 1790, Cozzi was able to make the justified claim that he had been responsible for substituting Venetian productions for imported Japanese and Chinese porcelain. He also claimed, with justice, that his ware was as good as the porcelain coming from Saxony.

Little is known of the artists responsible for modelling and decorating the Cozzi porcelain, but the names Ludovico Ortolani (born in 1732), Pietro Ortolani, Antonio Paroli, Carlo Fabri, Giovanni Maria Ortolani and the brothers Baccin are known. The Ortolani who worked for Cozzi is not to be confused with the different artist of the same name appearing on the Vezzi saucer in the British Museum. Most of Cozzi's artists were men enticed from a rival factory at Nove in the *Terra Ferma,* the establishment of Antonibon, mentioned earlier as having been given permission to produce porcelain in addition to Hewelcke.

It is suspected that Cozzi was not solely responsible for the success of his paste, and that he had the collaboration of the geologist G. B. Arduini who had made an exhaustive study of the caves and minerals in the Tretto district from where Cozzi drew his materials. Towards 1790, the Cozzi factory began to decline. In October of that year, Cozzi had to ask the Board of Trade for a renewal of his subsidy. The decline was due not to negligence or to a falling-off in the quality of the production. The unsettled conditions of impending war and revolution were affecting Italy as well as other parts of Europe. With the advance of Napoleon, the nobility and the rich, who had been Cozzi's best customers, were leaving Venice for more tranquil lands. With the abdication of the last doge in 1797, even the State ceased to support Cozzi. When first the French and later the Austrian authorities took over in Venice, orders for porcelain went to Sèvres and Vienna. The aging Cozzi tried to struggle on without patronage, but finally in 1812 he was forced to close.

Cozzi's porcelain was made of a hard paste, decidedly grey in tone, with a glistening glaze. The colours used included iron red, iridescent emerald green and violet. The gilding was exceptionally good, the gold being obtained from Venetian sequin coins. The factory mark, an anchor in iron red, is generally found on tableware; pieces of particularly high quality were marked with a gold anchor, while figures and groups were seldom marked in any way.

Cozzi decorations have all the charm of the Venetian landscape artists (Figs. 1 and 9), even if they are not quite so perfectly executed as the paintings on Meissen porcelain. Cozzi's output included much charming *Chinoiserie.* His figures and groups were particularly attractive and included mythological subjects, figures after engravings by Callot (Fig. 2) and the *Commedia dell'Arte.* Some of the best of Cozzi's productions reveal a strong Sèvres influence. A plate dated 1780, in the Victoria and Albert Museum, is a good example, with its dark blue borders, rich gilding and reserve panels with beautifully painted scenes (Fig. 4). The central panel depicts the story of Europa and the Bull, after Paolo Veronese, and the border panels consist of miniatures after the masterpieces of Tiepolo and Tintoretto in the Doges' Palace. Even so, Cozzi never fully achieved the beauty of Sèvres. Nevertheless, in his neo-classical wares, produced between 1780 and 1800, he showed a great talent for originality of design.

Fraudulent imitations of Cozzi ware are not common. Occasionally pieces with a Cozzi mark are to be found which resemble the styles of other manufacturers. These were not intended as fakes. They were made as replacements for broken sets by the Venetian factory to the specifications of the individual customer.

The final closure of the Cozzi factory brought to an end the contribution of the City of Venice to an epoch of ceramic history, leaving Meissen, Vienna, Sèvres and other European centres to carry on the creative tradition.

MUSEUMS AND COLLECTIONS

Venetian porcelain may be seen at the following:

GREAT BRITAIN

London:	British Museum Victoria and Albert Museum

ITALY

Naples:	Museo 'Duca di Martina' alla Floridiana
Turin:	Museo Civico
Venice:	Civico Museo Correr Fondazione Querini-Stampaglia

FURTHER READING

Le Porcellane Italiane by G. Morazzoni, Milan, 1960.

Italian Porcelain by E. A. Lane, London, 1954.

Le Porcellane di Venezia e delle Nove by Nino Barbantini, Venice, 1936.

Notes on Venetian Ceramics by W. R. Drake, London, 1868.

Seventeenth-Century Medals

Richard Falkiner

Derek Witty

Fig. 1 **The Sun,** *reverse of Pope Clement XI, by E. Hamerani, 1701. Diam. 4 ins.*
Fig. 2 ***Piazza of St. John Lateran,*** *reverse of Pope Innocent XII, 1693. Diam. 4 ins.*
Fig. 3 **Androcles,** *reverse of Pope Alexander VII, by F. Travani, 1659. Diam. 4 ins.*

Derek Witty

Fig. 4 ***St. Peter's,*** *reverse of Pope Alexander VII, by G. Morone, 1661. Diam. 3 ins.*
Fig. 5 **Christ,** *possibly by Rossi, mid-sixteenth century. Diam. $6\frac{1}{4}$ ins.*
Fig. 6 ***Emperor Nero,*** *French, seventeenth century. Diam. 4 ins.*

Derek Witty

The tradition of medals in the seventeenth century remained essentially the same as in the previous century and a half. However the style had evolved with painting and sculpture and many which bear a date can be used as art historical documents. Frequently these medals have an importance as portraits, a tradition which was unbroken since Pisanello – with his magnificent work of the Byzantine Emperor, John Palaeologus, of 1438 or 39 – revived the Roman practice of making portrait medals. Italian medals had a certain amount in common with contemporary French medals but not with those of the German states, the designs of which had clearly been influenced for some time previously by the disrupting forces of the Reformation. The subjects of the reverses of these medals mainly represent allegorical or religious scenes, often beautifully executed.

There is a broad division in the works of this time; those issued by or on behalf of the popes on the one hand, and those made for secular patrons on the other.

The papal medals were made in far greater quantity than the rest, as they were presumably given away at audiences or could be bought in the souvenir shops which were hardly less prevalent than they are today. These factors raise many problems concerning the correct attribution of papal medals and this may account for their lack of popularity with collectors at the present time. The main problem is that it was the practice to make sets of portrait medals of popes, with appropriate reverses, and hence many bear dates or are in a style not corresponding with that of their actual manufacture or design. In addition, earlier medals were cast, sometimes from struck originals, to satisfy the demand for medals which could no longer be supplied. Both these disadvantages can be overcome with careful study from the stylistic and technical points of view.

The difficulty of dating medals from dies

Of far greater complexity are the medals struck from dies. Obviously medals were made in much smaller quantities than coins, which were intended for general circulation. In the case of coins, the dies were used until they had been worn out, which would be fairly soon after making them; with medals this was usually not the case. Thus comparatively fresh dies were available for the striking of 'old' medals at a later date. It requires considerable experience to be sure of the period of manufacture of some of these pieces, but it could be argued that it is the date of the engraving of the dies rather than the actual striking which is important, provided that the metal used is similar in character to the artist's original intention.

The medals made on behalf of secular potentates were frequently similar in design but not universally so, and they tend to be larger and cast rather than struck. Those with portraits were made to be presented to the adherents of the noblemen concerned in much the same way as signed photographs were given and received by the aristocracy of the nineteenth and early twentieth centuries. At the same time, with the evolution of Humanism in the seventeenth century, it became the custom for virtually every *palazzo* to have its collection of medals together with its gems, natural curiosities and the like. It was these collections which gave rise to a variety of medals betraying a nostalgia for the classical past. These would have been made as a speculative venture. It seems that their owners were not concerned with the authenticity of these pieces, and there are quite a number of grotesque objects displaying a complete misunderstanding of the classics, passages of which they were made to satisfy.

The division between the religious and secular need not be taken as absolutely rigid since we must remember that the dignitaries of the Church were among the greatest scholars and collectors of their day. Thus many of the larger papal medals were commissioned by Vatican officials in their worldly capacity.

The architectural medals of all periods have a particular interest, none more so than seventeenth-century Italian examples. One of the most popular of these must be Gaspare Morone's medal (Fig. 4) which bears on its reverse Bernini's original idea for the piazza of St. Peter's. In this particular one we can see into the mind of an architect whose project materialised in a different way from his original conception.

It is always unsatisfactory to mention prices particularly in general terms, not least because they become dated very quickly; however it is safe to say that prices have risen very steeply and interest seems to be increasing while the supply must of necessity remain static.

MUSEUMS AND COLLECTIONS

Italian seventeenth-century medals may be seen at the following:

GREAT BRITAIN

Cambridge: Fitzwilliam Museum

London: British Museum
Victoria and Albert Museum

Oxford: Ashmolean Museum

U.S.A.

Brunswick: Bawdoin College Museum of Art.
Saton Collection, Maine

Washington: National Gallery of Art

FURTHER READING

The literature on the subject is extensive, although expensive and in many cases hard to come by; this is because of the minute classification involved, but at least the work has been done.

The Andrew Ciechanowiecki Collection (Exhibition Catalogue), J. B. Speed Art Museum, Louisville, Kentucky, 1969. Fully illustrated and catalogued in great detail, the biographical notes on the medallists are useful in the absence of Forrer (*op.cit.*). Complementary to Hill and Pollard.

Renaissance Medals from the Samuel H. Kress Collection at the National Gallery of Art by G. F. Hill and Graham Pollard, London, 1967.

A Biographical Dictionary of Medallists, 8 Vols, by L. Forrer, London, 1904–30. Very useful often with lists of the complete *oeuvre* of an artist but out of print and very expensive.

Les Médailleurs Italiens by A. Armand, Paris, 1883–87. The standard work.

7

A. C. Cooper

Fig. 7 ***Francesco Redi*** *by Massimiliano Soldani-Benzi (1658–1740), 1684. Diam.* $3\frac{1}{8}$ *ins. Francesco Redi (1626?–1697/98) was a famous Italian naturalist and poet who was personal physician to the Grand Duke of Tuscany.*
Fig. 8 ***Aere Perennius,*** *reverse of the above medal. (Heim Gallery.)*
(Figs. 1–6 *Andrew Ciechanowiecki Collection.*)

8

A. C. Cooper

Furniture for the Canal Palaces

Phillis Rogers

1

Fig. 1 **Dressing-glass**, *Venetian, eighteenth century. Painted and gilt wood, height 2 ft. 9 ins. In addition to their elaborate carving, Venetian rococo pieces were often covered with a profusion of painted flowers and shell motifs. (Victoria and Albert Museum, London.)*

Venetian furniture during the eighteenth century grew out of stiff formal ostentation into a style of exaggerated delicacy and frivolity

The baroque furniture of Venice is little different from that produced elsewhere in Italy. As much influenced as Roman architecture of the period by Bernini (1598–1680) and Borromini (1599–1667), the great baroque architects, it is characterised by classical motifs – acanthus leaves, heavy volutes and pillars. The effect of the furniture is bold in form as well as rich in colour.

Palaces were laid out with the reception-rooms on the first floor, or *piano nobile*. These were furnished with majestic carved tables with marble tops and embellished with examples of antique and contemporary sculpture. They were chilly, formal rooms and families would lead their private lives above, on the mezzanine floor. Here the furniture was relatively simple, usually of walnut and not gilt. Few contemporary accounts of these rooms exist since visitors were overwhelmed by the splendour of the reception-rooms; only a few examples of the furniture have survived as it was not thought to be of much consequence.

In the seventeenth century the renaissance *cassone* gave way to the *armadio*, or wardrobe, and the *credenza*, which was a form of side-board with built-in cupboards. These were characterised by architectural features and were rectangular and symmetrical in shape, later in the century taking on a serpentine profile. One of the most important pieces of furniture was the cabinet-on-stand, the supports of which were frequently in the form of caryatids. The cabinets above resembled palaces, displaying broken pediments, columns and sculptured figures in niches. These were intended to hold collections of small objects, such as medals or curiosities; one such was described by John Evelyn in his diary which contained lumps of petrified substances, including a hedgehog. The cabinets were very ornate, their façades embellished with all kinds of rare and lustrous materials – precious and semi-precious stones *(pietre dure)* and ivory and metal inlays.

Evelyn also describes a bed he saw inlaid with agate, crystals, cornelians, and lapis lazuli. He notes that most of the beds were made from gilt wrought iron, but few survive today.

In the second half of the century it was usual for state beds to be draped with heavy velvet hangings after the French fashion. This influence from the Court of Louis XIV, which was itself derived from Italy, spread throughout the Venetian furnishings fashionable at this time. The designs of Bérain, Marot and Lepautre began to circulate in Italy and Venetian patricians attempted to imitate the grandeur of Versailles. It became almost *de rigueur* for furniture in state apartments to be gilt. Here, the overriding factor was the sumptuousness of the pieces rather than their utility. Chairs developed into articles designed to display the carver's virtuosity, which led a visiting Frenchman to complain that he was unable to find an armchair in which he could sit, due to the refinement of the carving.

Perhaps the most renowned piece of Venetian furniture, the popularity of which carried on well into the eighteenth century is the pedestal figure stand, frequently of a life-size Moor painted in bright polychrome colours and designed to carry an Oriental porcelain vase. The outstanding exponent of the carver's art in the production of these figures was the wood-carver Andrea Brustolon (1662–1732), probably the most skilled craftsman of his age. He devoted most of his career to carving ecclesiastical pieces, but he did turn his hand to creating articles for domestic use. He was born in the little town of Belluno in the Veneto; his father, also a carver by trade, soon recognised his son's talent and sent him to Venice to be apprenticed under a Genoese sculptor. After this training the young Brustolon journeyed to Rome where he was profoundly struck by the high baroque achievements of Bernini. His style never changed thereafter, and his works of the eighteenth century never lost their resemblance to work of the previous century.

His influence is clearly visible in the designs of William Kent (1684–1748), and indeed a pair of console-tables, formerly in Stoneleigh Abbey, Warwickshire, and now ascribed to Brustolon, were once thought to be by the Englishman. His most famous work is the suite of furniture, now in the

2

A. C. Cooper

Fig. 2 **Armchair,** *from a set of three chairs and a sofa, Venetian, eighteenth century. Much Italian furniture of the eighteenth century is painted in pastel colours, unlike French rococo pieces of similar design with their delicate gilding. Cane-work was popular for seat furniture. (Christie, Manson and Woods Ltd., London.)*

3

Angelo Hornak

Fig. 3 ***Commode with matching looking-glass.*** *Venetian, eighteenth century. Green lacquer-work with* chinoiserie *gilt designs and marble top, height of commode 3 ft., width 4½ ft., height of glass 6 ft. 2 ins. The vogue for Chinese lacquer furniture all over Europe during the eighteenth century led to superb* chinoiserie *pieces such as this commode. (Ca' Rezzonico, Venice.)*

Fig. 4 **Commode,** *Venetian, eighteenth century. Yellow lacquer with gilding and painted flowers, height 2 ft. 11 ins., width $4\frac{1}{2}$ ft.*
This bulbously top-heavy commode, attractive despite its exaggerated proportions, exemplifies the height of the rococo style in Venice.
(Ca' Rezzonico.)

Fig. 5 **Commode,** *one of a pair, Venetian, mid-eighteenth century. Painted wood, width 2 ft. 5 ins.*
Lock-plates and handles on Venetian furniture were almost invariably carved in wood and gilt, rather than made of gilt cast-metal, as was usual throughout the rest of Europe. Often the key, as here, served as the only handle to a drawer.
(Sotheby and Co., London.)

Ca' Rezzonico, Venice, which the Venier family commissioned from him. This undertaking took him some twenty years to execute and was completed at the end of the century. It comprises over forty pieces of which the largest, an elaborate console-table, is signed; a very rare occurrence in Venetian furniture. He chose to carve these articles in ebony and boxwood, both hard woods, with a resulting crispness not found in the work of his imitators, since in general Venetian carving was executed in soft woods such as pine.

Brustolon's style is characterised by a feeling for naturalism, which frees him from the stylised conventions of the Baroque. In one of the armchairs in the Venier suite, the arms are supported by two Moorish figures standing on realistic tree-stumps round which a convolvulus twines its tendrils. The sources of his decoration are various – mythological, allegorical and rustic.

This independence of convention is not shared by the other great furniture carver, Antonio Corradini (1668–1752), who is best known for his marble statues. He, too, interpreted his designs as works of art rather than as utilitarian objects. He was less original than Brustolon and confined himself to the

6

7

Fig. 6 **Sofa,** *one of a set of four (two large and two, as this one, small), Venetian, eighteenth century. Walnut, length 7 ft. 10 ins., height 3 ft. 2 ins. Still standing in the position for which it was originally designed, the sofa illustrated here is of the type found in formal reception-rooms. (Ca' Rezzonico.)*

Fig. 7 **Sofa,** *Venetian, eighteenth century. Gilt wood and silk, length 6 ft. 5 ins., height 4 ft. 9 ins. The flowing line of this magnificent sofa, its delicate decoration and elaborate gilding all illustrate the influence of French furniture on that of Venice. (Ca' Rezzonico.)*

vocabulary of the Baroque, creating an elegant and courtly effect. Although he carried on working into the rococo period he modified his style very little, retaining the feeling for grandeur of the former style whilst making minor concessions to the new by way of asymmetrical *rocaille* motifs. In his carving he excelled in the portrayal of playful *putti* and *amorini* which prance among the thick foliage and scrolls.

The work of Corradini brings us into the eighteenth century and the rococo period. It was not until the middle years of the century that this French style found favour with the Venetians, who until then had continued to express their desire for richness in the baroque manner. But slowly the tenor of life began to modify itself, and by 1741 Lady Mary Wortley Montagu, a resident in Venice for some twenty years, was writing to her daughter that 'the manners of Italy are so much changed since we were here last, the alteration is scarcely credible . . . The French, being masters, introduced all their customs, which were eagerly embraced by the ladies'.

Still politically free, unlike the rest of Italy, and although economically on the decline, Venice had the most effervescent society in Europe, which was reflected in the theatre and opera and captured on the canvases of Guardi (1712–93) and Pietro Longhi (1702–85). Venice was a city of carnivals and masques and each evening patricians and the wealthy bourgeoisie would go to the Ridotto, where many fortunes were won and gambled away. Every grand lady had a *casino*, which was either a little summer-house or else a suite of intimate rooms, where she entertained her friends, attended by her *cicisbeo* (gallant). Even when the Venetians retired to the country on what they termed the *villeggiatura* (country residence), the lavish entertainments continued, and were aped by the more prosperous of the middle class who built themselves villas alongside the fashionable Brenta Canal.

Their frivolous ways were reflected in their furnishings. Instead of the stately flavour of the Baroque, the rococo style, promoted through the designs of Pillement (1728–1808), Pineau (1684–1754) and others, shunned rectilinear forms and sharp angles, favouring instead a flowing curvaceous line and asymmetrical shapes. Classical motifs made way for *rocaille* and shell ornaments, and above all a great enthusiasm was shown for sprays of flowers, which are even known to have been painted on kitchen ceilings.

Furniture of this period is typified by its showy, colourful appearance, and it should be judged by this rather than by the quality of its construction, which was often very shoddy; interiors and backs rarely received the meticulous care revealed in contemporary English work. The guilds helped to maintain a certain standard of craftsmanship in furniture made in Venice, but their authority did not extend over the surrounding region.

The passion for clear, lively colours resulted in the production of much lacquered furniture, which was painted on a gesso ground and then varnished. Like the rest of Europe, Venice in the latter half of the seventeenth century was captivated by the Orient, and fashionable households were eager to display Chinese lacquer, or failing this the European version called 'japan'. Venetian japan, according to Maximilian Misson, was by 1688 'much esteemed' and could be bought at all prices. It was used to ornament all manner of objects from large *armadi* to small toilet-boxes and trays.

At first the decorative motifs closely followed the Oriental prototypes (Fig. 3) but in the eighteenth century the Venetians delighted in decorating their furniture with bunches of flowers (Fig. 4), views of the lagoon and pastoral scenes as well as with *chinoiseries* which continued to be popular; these quaint figures echoed in their antics the light-hearted Venetian life (Fig. 10). Black backgrounds favoured in the seventeenth century were thought too sombre; instead, lacquered articles were painted with bright and pastel hues, which, sadly, have dulled, due to the aging of the varnish. These colours were offset by the gold of the carved gilt framing reliefs, which were employed instead of the gilt-bronze mounts found on French furniture. Even keyhole escutcheons were carved in wood, although drawer-handles, where present, were sometimes cast from gilt metal. When they were omitted the key doubled in function as a handle (Fig. 5).

So popular was this means of decoration that a cheap substitute for the less wealthy was developed called *arte povera*, which became a pastime for

Fig. 8 ***Two chairs** from a set of twelve, Venetian, mid-eighteenth century. Painted decoration. (Mallet and Son Ltd., London.)*

Fig. 9 ***Detail from 'The Toilet'** by Pietro Longhi (1702–85), Venice, c.1760; showing a* trespolo, *or tripod stand. (Civico Museo Correr, Venice.)*

Fig. 10 ***Lacquered bureau,** Venetian, eighteenth century. Decorated with* arte povera *maritime and pastoral scenes, width 3 ft. 7 ins. (Christie's.)*

patrician ladies (Fig. 10). Instead of painting a design, coloured cut-out prints, some of which were published specifically for this purpose by Remondini of Bassano, were stuck on the gesso ground and varnished. Prints applied in this way were designed by well-known artists such as Zuccarelli (1702–88). Indeed, Venetian interior furnishings at this time had a close relationship with the fine arts and this collaboration is seen in a pair of lacquered *chinoiserie* doors in the Ca' Rezzonico attributed to Giambattista Tiepolo (1696–1770), who is known to have painted several ceilings in the palace.

Furniture other than lacquered ware was usually made in walnut (Fig. 6), but rarely in mahogany which was more expensive since its import was highly taxed. Veneering was little employed, but where executed was only undertaken by the top category of furniture-makers.

Either lacquered or in carved walnut, one of the most typical pieces of Venetian furniture was the swollen-sided, or *bombé* commode (Fig. 4). This usually had two drawers and occasionally contained cupboards in the sides. Often it was flanked by a pair of smaller, inverted-pear-shaped commodes, made *en suite* (Fig. 5). Little tripod stands with serpentine stems called *trespoli* complemented the arrangement (Fig. 9).

Above commodes and over chimney-pieces it was common to find mirrors ornamented with rococo carvings (Fig. 3). The Venetians had shown an enthusiasm for mirrors since the sixteenth century and they had formed an integral part of baroque interiors. With technical improvements, huge sheets of glass could now be manufactured so that rococo mirrors attained vast dimensions.

This love of mirrors helped to produce the light impression of rococo interiors, further enhanced by the soft coloured silks and chintzes preferred to the heavy, dark brocades and velvets of the previous period.

Chairs were many and various, according to their function. They included the exaggerated settees (Fig. 6) of the ballroom and saloon, some of which seated up to ten people; the comfortable *bergère* armchair of French inspiration; and the side-chair decorated with an interlaced figure-of-eight on the back, a recurring motif on Venetian chairbacks. A great many chairs, especially designed for summer villas, were upholstered in cane (Fig. 2). This feeling for utility and fitness is repeated in the bookcase secretaires which clearly owe much to English design in their outline. Indeed, just as the English were impressed by the Venetian furnishings they saw on the Grand Tour, so Venice developed an admiration for those from England. Lady Mary Wortley Montagu noted that by 1756 'in general all the shops are full of English merchandise, and they boast of everything coming from London in the same style as they used to do from Paris'.

This was an enduring influence into the neo-classical period when Hepplewhite-inspired chairs were in vogue. The neo-classical style which Europe embraced in the second half of the eighteenth century took a long time to gain acceptance in Venice, and when it did in the last quarter of the century, the spirit of the Rococo was still in evidence.

Ignoring the cold, correct neo-Classicism of the Romans, realised in gold and white, Venice chose to apply classical decoration of a delicate and colourful nature, introducing flowers and ribbons of the type which delighted Marie Antoinette. Venice only adopted those motifs prompted by the excavations of Pompeii and Herculaneum after the fall of the republic (1797), under the domination of Napoleon.

8

Mallet & Son Photo

9

Hamlyn Ltd.

10

Christie's Photo

MUSEUMS AND COLLECTIONS

Venetian furniture of the eighteenth century may be seen at the following:

GREAT BRITAIN

London: Victoria and Albert Museum

ITALY

Venice: Ca' Rezzonico
Civico Museo Correr

FURTHER READING

Lacche veneziane settecentesche by Saul Levy, Milan, 1967.

Il mobile veneziano del settecento by G. Morazzoni, Milan, 1958.

A History of Italian Furniture by W. Odom, New York, 1919.

Collector's Corner

James Barry

Engraver of The Grand Manner in Miniature

James Barry, R.A. (1741-1806), native of Cork, student in Dublin, Paris and Rome, and for the last thirty-five years of his life an undoubtedly Irish Londoner, was **the principal champion of 'high art' in late eighteenth-century England.** Through writings and lectures he endeavoured to persuade his fellow artists and potential patrons that painting should wherever possible recall the heroic virtues of Antiquity, teach the truths of religion and celebrate the triumphs of a new and, as he hoped, 'truly Greek' period of progress, liberty and taste.

His gospel proved immensely popular but few could afford to pay him to put it into practice. Private collectors generally preferred portraiture, especially if done by Barry's associate, Reynolds (himself a believer in the doctrine of 'high art'). They were unwilling to provide the wall space for the great schemes which Barry proposed, or to risk an association which might provoke his fits of 'temper like insanity', under which even such firm friends as Edmund Burke and Joseph Nollekens suffered.

Barry's one opportunity came in 1777 when the Society of Arts accepted his offer to decorate the walls of their newly built meeting room in the Adelphi with 'a series of pictures analogous to the views of the institution.' For the next five years Barry worked hard at the scheme and by 1782 had produced six canvases—four measuring 11 feet 10 inches x 15 feet 2 inches and two 11 feet 10 inches x 42 feet—illustrating the *Progress of Human Knowledge* from the time of *Orpheus* to *Elysium, The State of Final Retribution.* The paintings and the painter became famous and, until well into the nineteenth century, London guide books listed Barry's Adelphi pictures as one of the sights to see. **Fame, however, did not bring further commissions for the artist** and, to raise funds, he invited subscriptions for engravings of the paintings; in 1791, he published engravings of all six paintings and between 1793 and 1800 he brought out a further seven prints showing enlarged details.

Unlike most painters of the period, Barry preferred to etch the plates himself than to give the work to a professional engraver. He took great care in representing the scale of the original paintings so that in prints which at their largest extend only to 1 foot 4½ inches x 3 feet, a real feeling of the grand manner is preserved. **He used sweeping lines and impressionistic cross-hatching in a style which was to influence his admirer Blake.** Often, at the bottom of the engravings, he wrote in his own nervous handwriting an appropriate quotation or motto.

He was cross with subscribers who complained of this roughness of technique, and, though he needed the money they offered him for his works, he could not bear to be seen canvassing for it. Once the sculptor Nollekens called out in front of others: 'Well, Jem, I have been very successful for you this week—I have got you three more subscribers for your prints.' It is said that Barry 'bade him with an oath, mind his own affairs—if the Nobility wanted his engravings, they knew where he was to be found'. Today, his prints are worth seeking out, not only for their decorative effect and intrinsic artistic merit but also for their association with the strange personality of their creator.

There has been such a concentration of scholarly writing on the work of Reynolds and Romney that **it is only recently that interest has centered around such lesser-known artists as Barry.** Many print-shops, notably those in the British Museum area of London, carry engravings by artists like J. H. Mortimer (1740-1779) or Giles Hussey (1710-1788). Although drawings by Barry

Top: The Diagorides Victors at Olympia, 1791. Centre: The Thames or the Triumph of Navigation, 1791. Bottom: Orpheus instructing the savage people in Theology, 1791.

K. Hoddle

do not often come on the market, it is still possible to pick up engravings of his Adelphi paintings for a comparatively modest sum. In good condition, they fetch as much as £30, while £10-£18 is a reasonable price to pay for those in fair condition.

DAVID ALLAN

DEATH OF VENICE

The same natural features which made the area of the lagoon attractive to its first settlers as a refuge from Attila the Hun are now threatening Venice's continued existence as a human settlement. In November 1966 the north of Italy was inundated. Luckily, there was not a heavy loss of life, but the damage to buildings was enormous. At the time, it was the situation in Florence which was most critical and which attracted most attention and relief effort. But in Venice the disaster was also great; the heavy rains coincided with the *acqua alta*, an unusually high tide, the incidence of which has been more frequent in recent years. Out of 59 submersions of over 3½ feet in the past hundred years, 49 have taken place in the past thirty-six years and 30 in the last ten. It is difficult to account for this trend, and large sums of money will have to be spent on research and experiment.

Dangerous Conditions

Basically there are four conditions in the northern Adriatic which affect the situation: tides, marine currents, the *sirocco*—a warm south wind which sometimes blows for three days on end—and the so-called 'seiches'. The last expression describes an oscillatory motion which occurs five or six times a year from end to end of the lagoon. If these four conditions should operate at maximum intensity simultaneously, Venice would be practically submerged under nine feet of muddy, oily water.

Water and Air Pollution

Apart from the threat of apocalyptic catastrophe there is the daily deterioration of buildings, statues and paintings. The combination of the salt water and the corrosive smoke blowing across from the industrial plants on the mainland has already stolen a march on those whose Sisyphean task it is to preserve the treasures of Venice.

Lack of Technical Facilities

Until March 1968 one of the main obstacles to the work of preservation in Venice was the lack of technical facilities. In 1778 the Republic set up a 'public restoration laboratory' in one of the refectories of the monastery of SS. Giovanni and Paolo; but in 1797, when the city fell to Napoleon, the Republic ceased and the French authorities ordered the closing of the laboratory. Since then, only *in situ* restoration of painting and sculpture was possible until 1955, when, thanks to the generosity of the Cararetto family, facilities were set up in a large hall of the Villa Garzoni at Pontecasale. But this was 70 kilometres from Venice and risks were involved in transporting fragile works of art to and from so distant a point. The inundation of November 1966 spurred the authorities into action and at last, in the disused church of San Gregorio, beside Santa Maria della Salute, Venice was provided with a laboratory equipped in the most modern way and capable of accommodating even the largest of Venetian canvases. Substantial contributions to the cost were made by the Americans, the Germans and the Dutch.

To preserve Venice, both the city and its works of art, has been, is and will continue to be an enormously expensive operation.

WINTER SIGHT-SEEING IN ROME

If anyone tried to tie the baroque style to a particular location, his first choice would have to be Rome. If you wish to follow up Martin Meade's article (on page 1821), you could start there.

Most people would never think of visiting Italy in the winter but it is then that it is most pleasant, for the hordes of tourists have long since departed and the heat has given way to much milder weather.

To see all the treasures of baroque Rome would take many months but much can be done in a day. Where better to start than **St. Peter's—the grandest visual statement of the counter-reformation which engendered the Baroque.** Here Michelangelo's dome and Maderno's façade enclose the dynamic sculptural work of Bernini. Outside, the giant colonnades around the *piazza* symbolise the all-embracing arms of the Church and on the right rises the *Scala Regia*, the staircase to the Vatican.

Across the *Ponte S. Angelo* and one is not far from **the Piazza Navona where the dramatic façade of Borromini's Sta. Agnese in Agone and Bernini's Four Rivers fountain greet the eye.** The rivalry between the two artists is unambiguously stated here in the figure of the Nile which has its face covered in order not to see the Borromini façade. Behind the *piazza* lies **S. Ivo alla Sapienza,** Borromini's masterpiece of geometry.

Eastwards down narrow streets and one arrives at **S. Andrea al Quirnale** where Bernini brought a sense of baroque grandeur to a small space. A few paces away lies Borromini's **S. Carlo alla Quattro Fontane.** Virtually next door is **S. Maria della Vittoria** and there one can see the full illusionism of Bernini's *Sta. Teresa.*

The visitor can conclude his tour at the **Palazzo Barberini,** where the combined efforts of Bernini and Borromini offset Cortona's magnificent ceiling.

DUBLIN

Despite the ravages of progress, Dublin is still one of the most attractive cities in the British Isles. Although the Irish Tourist Office are happy to give any information about guided tours or what to see in Dublin, readers who have not been able to obtain official brochures may find the appended list of some use.

The Bank of Ireland, College Green, is one of the most striking Georgian buildings in Dublin. Begun in 1729 by Sir Edward Pearce to house the Irish Parliament, it is surmounted by fine statues by Edward Smyth.

Trinity College, College Green, contains two of the most attractive buildings by Sir William Chambers; what is now the public examination hall completed in 1791, and the chapel built in 1798. The mid-eighteenth-century library contains illuminated gospels of which the Book of Durrow is the oldest and the Book of Kells the most famous.

The Civic Museum in Coppinger Row is another attractive Georgian house built for the Society of Artists in 1765 and now containing work by Irish artists of the last two centuries.

The Huguenot Cemetery in Merrion Row reflects the cosmopolitan character of early eighteenth-century Dublin. There are fine monuments to Catholics and Jews as well as Protestants.

St. Stephen's Green, famous in Irish literature, retains the beauty of its Georgian gardens, although most of the original buildings have been rebuilt or added to.

The Mansion House, 19 Dawson Street, was the headquarters of the Royal Irish Academy and contains fine plasterwork and fireplaces.

Kildare Street contains **The National Library, The National Museum** and the Parliament Building, the **Dail,** formerly Leinster House. The museum contains one of the finest collections of early Christian art.

Merrion Square, the most famous in Dublin, dates from 1762. Many of the great figures in Irish literature and politics lived there, from the Duke of Wellington to Oscar Wilde and W. B. Yeats.

Ely Place is perhaps the least spoilt of the surviving areas of Georgian Dublin.

The National Gallery of Ireland is one of the most outstanding small galleries in Europe, with a fine collection of French and Italian paintings.

Dublin Castle, despite its historical interest, is architecturally undistinguished, having suffered heavily from Victorian restoration. The State Apartments are magnificent and the Heraldic Museum contains interesting relics of Ireland's dramatic history.

St. Wesburgh's Church in Castle Street has a particularly fine interior belied by the severity of its Palladian front.

Christ Church Cathedral in Winetavern Street lost almost all its early features to the clumsy good intentions of Victorian restorers.

St. Patrick's Cathedral contains one of the best collections of monuments in the British Isles including the graves of Jonathan Swift and the Duke of Schomberg.

St. Audoen's Church in the High Street is the oldest parish church in Dublin, parts of which date back to the twelfth century.

O'Connell Street (formerly Sackville Street) used to be one of the finest streets in the capital but it has been heavily redeveloped in recent years. Of all the handsome buildings it once contained, **The Gate Theatre** and **The Rotunda Hospital** are the two most interesting survivors.

Parnell's Square contains some very fine Georgian houses of which **Charlemont House**, built by Sir William Chambers in 1762, is the most interesting. It now houses an interesting collection of modern French and English paintings.

No list of buildings to see in Dublin could stand without mention of the **Custom House** in Abbey Street, which is one of the most magnificent late eighteenth-century buildings in Ireland. Satiated with weariness from architectural splendour, the tourist may find refuge and relaxation in the beauty of **Phoenix Park**.

Market Trends

THE ARTS AND WEAPONS OF INDIA

Most of the Indian artefacts which appear in London antique shops and auction rooms are the result of a hundred years of haggling and buying by soldiers and civilians of the British administration in India. At one end of the scale, wealthy and discriminating buyers brought back fine carpets, bronzes and jade; at the other end, cheap trinkets, ornaments and weapons were the objects which came back from the Raj in the baggage of Tommy Atkins. Many of these items were copied in England. Chairs, brass trays and fretted wooden tables were made in very large numbers, besides other equally ornate but far less practical pieces. The surfeit of 'Indian styles' must have something to do with the fact that interest in Indian works of art has, until quite recently, been restricted to those with a specialist knowledge of the country and its culture.

Weapons

Exceptions to this pattern are Indian swords and other hand-weapons. Jewelled swords and daggers were given as presents to officials of the East India Company in the eighteenth century, and increasing military involvement in India made England familiar with their weapons and designs. These often magnificent weapons have been widely collected by arms and armour enthusiasts for over a hundred years. A carved jade dagger-hilt, with the pommel carved in the shape of a horse's head, the eyes set with *cabochon* rubies in gold collets, was sold for £85 at Sotheby's early in 1970. This piece was recognisably eighteenth-century, but a *katar,* or punch dagger, with a hilt chiselled with leaves and a gold damascened finish sold for only £22 because it was demonstrably nineteenth-century. Weapons of this sort are collected either for the rich ornament of the hilts or for the high quality and finish of the blade. Many of the items that do not have any special characteristic make very little money at auction. Two *tulwars* (sabres) with attractively chiselled hilts, *c.* 1840, sold for only £12 at Sotheby's last year in a lot with two Brown Bess socket bayonets. Shields were among the most highly decorated items of Indian armour, and they attract high prices at auction. A fine buffalo-hide shield, the surface painted brown and decorated in gold with four panels of wild beasts fighting, separated by four green glass bosses, centred on a medallion decorated with a head, sold for £55 at Sotheby's in 1971.

Rugs and Carpets

Indian rugs and carpets have never attracted the frenzied attention given to those from Persia and Turkey, or from the Khanates of Russian Asia. In the last five or six years, however, there has been a tendency to pay more attention to the products of Afghanistan and India. Articles of the highest quality, of course, have always done well in salerooms, but mediocre or unremarkable items from India have never done as well as their equivalents from Persia or Turkey, at least until this newfound interest developed. In 1970, two Tabriz rugs from Persia, 6 feet 7 inches by 4 feet 9 inches, sold for £480 at Christie's. Earlier in the year, two Agra rugs from India, 7 feet 8 inches by 4 feet 1 inch, fetched only £170 at Sotheby's, despite their excellent condition.

Glass-Paintings and Bronzes

Indian glass-paintings make only the rarest appearance in London salerooms. Five paintings of youths accompanied by girls, either seated or standing by trees and shrubs, sold for £28 at Sotheby's in 1970, and a similar set, depicting young girls at play, sold for £40. They appear so seldom that it is hardly fair to attach a label to these prices, still less establish any distinct trend. Bronzes, on the other hand, appear frequently in salerooms. A south Indian bronze figure of Ganesha seated on a lotus throne, described in the Sotheby's catalogue as 'four-armed and holding his various attributes', sold for £50 in 1970, in a lot with a figure of Lakshmi and two other images. These very attractive ornaments are probably a good investment today.

DAMASCUS HOBNAIL

IRISH SILVER, FURNITURE AND GLASS

Irish porringer by A. Sinclair, Dublin, 1708, sold at Sotheby's for £2,100 in 1971.

Irish silver is still basically an Irish interest and the prices lag behind those paid for good London pieces, although they are probably higher than those paid for English provincial silver. Occasionally, however, a truly exceptional piece will come on to the market and then an extremely large sum will be paid. A good example of this was the Royal Queen Anne helmet-shaped ewer by Thomas Bolton, Dublin, 1702, which was engraved with the Queen's full armorials and was sold for £7,000 at Sotheby's in June 1969; as far as is known, this is the highest price ever paid at auction for a piece of Irish silver.

In general, most pieces still fetch below £1,000 at auction and a number of small pieces, strawberry-dishes, mugs, cups, casters and the like which the Irish makers appear to have specially favoured, can be purchased for between £200 and £600. One characteristic feature of Irish silver is its chasing, which is often referred to as 'Irish Rococo'. It is unlike anything produced in England, with its use of animal, bird, fruit and foliage motifs mixed together and although it is often a little diffuse, at its best such as in the work of the mid-eighteenth-century Dublin maker John Williamson it can be very attractive.

Pieces made in the smaller towns are naturally of some rarity, and when they do appear on the market they can be expected to fetch more than pieces of equivalent quality from the large cities. A famous example of this was a small mug by J. or W. Wall, *c.* 1710, which was made at Kinsale, in County Cork. Only a handful of pieces from this source are known and this particular example fetched £340 in 1967. Today it would probably be worth double this sum, while a Dublin mug of similar quality would be unlikely to fetch much more than £350.

During the nineteenth century, Irish silver closely followed English hybrid styles but lacked much of the sheer technical virtuosity which makes English Victorian silver so extraordinary. However, a finely chased piece does appear occasionally; one example is the Freedom Box by the highly skilled craftsman Edward Murray, Dublin, 1822, which was sold for the surprisingly high sum of £520 in 1967.

Furniture

Irish furniture, with its distinctive rococo carvings, appears regularly but in small quantities on the market. Tables which have the usual lion-mask-centred frieze are always described as 'Irish', but the main problem is that so little is known about Irish furniture by many of the smaller salerooms that many pieces which are unquestionably Irish do not get catalogued as such. This gives the impression that fewer pieces are sold than is actually the case. Irish furniture tends to be heavier and less elegant than its English equivalent and usually dates from the George II period. In general, it fetches rather less than English examples of comparable quality.

Cut and Moulded Glass

Irish cut glass of the late eighteenth century is currently out of fashion and is therefore well worth collecting. It is generally heavier, darker and cut with larger facets than English glass. Even very good pieces rarely fetch more than about £120 and can be bought for as little as £50. Another type of glass is early nineteenth-century moulded glass mainly in the form of jugs and decanters engraved with swags and floral wreaths. These pieces can also be bought inexpensively, £50-£100 being the price range.

KEITH POWNETT

GLASS, FURNITURE AND MAIOLICA OF ITALY

The fragility and rarity of Italian glass have combined to make this art form a field mainly for the discerning but patient collector. So when Sotheby's sold the Walker F. Smith collection in July 1968, interest was shown in many quarters. A fine Venetian goblet with flared bowl, hollow conical foot and decorated with spiral bands of white *latticinio* and dating from the seventeenth century, made £110 and a tall wine glass with a ribbed funnel bowl fetched £58. This type of glass was very thinly blown and the proportion of damaged pieces is high; it indicates the desire of the craftsman to produce glass for decoration rather than for practical use. Prices have risen over the last few years, aided by the magnificent exhibition at the British Museum in 1968—as well conceived and well organised a display as I have ever seen in England.

Furniture

The furniture of this period is restricted to *cassone, credenze,* chairs and bedsteads, and if the market sees some rarity such as the throne of Guiliano dei Medici, finely inlaid and carved, then the price of £6,300 paid in May 1967 at the Cornbury House Sale does not seem excessive. Fifteenth-century painted *cassone*

A sixteenth-century tazza painted by Francesco Xanto Avelli, showing Hector and Achilles, sold by Christie's in June 1969 for 1,100 guineas.

Photo: Christie, Manson & Woods

have long been held in esteem and when the Holford Collection was dispersed at Sotheby's in 1924, a particularly fine example depicting the story of *Tarquin and Lucretia* fetched £1,365 while a less good one of *Pluto and Proserpine* made £462. More recently, a walnut and parcel-gilt *cassone* realised 3,500 guineas in May 1968 and a seven foot wide walnut *credenza* was sold for 1,400 guineas on the same day at Christie's.

Italian Maiolica

The bold simplicity of form and the bright colours of Italian maiolica have long attracted the English collector; even the economic depression of 1930 did not deter an intrepid purchaser from paying £336 for a large Deruta dish painted with a phoenix and the coat-of-arms of the Raniere family of Perugia. Today there may be more discerning academic discussion as to the merits of a piece but rarity, provenance and condition determine its price. Over the last few years Italian dealers and collectors have shown themselves zealous to buy back the best items. A fine though damaged dish probably from Faenza painted with the arms of Pope Pius IV (Giovanni dei Medici, 1559-1565) in yellow, ochre and blue, was sold for only 250 guineas in May 1970, while in the same sale, a Deruta charger in perfect condition depicting a bust-length portrait of a girl (unidentified) in turquoise, yellow and ochre made 600 guineas. It is unusual for a Faenza *albarello* to be known to have come from a particular *farmacia* or drug store, but this was true of a fine example from the pharmacy of Orsini Colonna, one of a well-known series, and it realised 1,600 guineas at Christie's. *Tondini* were used predominantly in the elaborate architectural decoration of the time and therefore served little practical purpose. A good Urbino *istoriato tondino* of about 1545 showing *St. Paul in Malta* with ships and sea in the background made £600 at Sotheby's in March 1970.

TOM MILNES-GASKELL

18TH-CENTURY ITALIAN ANTIQUES

It is only during the last decade that Venetian furniture has attracted a wide public; this audience in the main consists of Italians who are desirous of buying back examples which form part of their national heritage. This interest is of course not only confined to furniture but to all things Italian. And during the last few years Italian dealers have been very active in the major European salerooms. While much Venetian furniture shows little quality of workmanship, it has an undeniable and often frivolous charm. This is well expressed by *torchères* (candlestands), the stems formed as blackamoors. A pair modelled as Nubians dating from the second quarter of the eighteenth century from Lord Wharton's collection realised £3,675 in 1970.

Furniture

Because of the underlying scarcity of Venetian furniture and the continuing demand, copies are made today in the eighteenth-century taste which have been known to fool the expert. This explains the emphasis on provenance in determining the authenticity of a piece. It is as well to remember that Venice in the eighteenth century had only a population of about 140,000 and produced only enough furniture for her own needs in addition to the small quantity that was brought by the Grand Tourists. Four attractively painted armchairs of the mid-century fetched the enormously inflated price of £4,725 in 1970. Not all Venetian furniture was painted; a walnut bureau cabinet inlaid with simple panels of marquetry was sold for £2,100 in 1969.

Vezzi and Cozzi Porcelain

The Vezzi factory at Venice survived for only seven years, 1720-1727, and as such its porcelain is among the rarest from eighteenth-century factories. Indeed only about one hundred and fifty pieces are known to exist. A Vezzi tea-bowl and saucer came up at Sotheby's in 1964 and fetched £330. A more important piece was included in a Christie's sale in 1968. It was a previously unrecorded *chinoiserie* bullet-shaped teapot (see illustration); the base was marked 'Vena' in red, and it realised £3,045. Later on in the century, when the factory was being run by Cozzi, the output was far more prolific, but most of what was produced has remained in Venice and the rest of Italy. Cozzi porcelain makes infrequent appearances on the London market. A rare pair of Cozzi tea-bowls and saucers deftly painted with the arms of Principe Giovanni of Venice realised £231 at Christie's in December 1969—a price justified by the fine quality of painting. More frequently to be seen at auction are figures; a pair of white figures of dwarfs shown as dancing women and indifferently modelled fetched £110 in 1968. A more attractive *chinoiserie* figure of a child in a long flowered skirt painted in green, puce and red in the same sale also fetched £110.

TOM MILNES-GASKELL

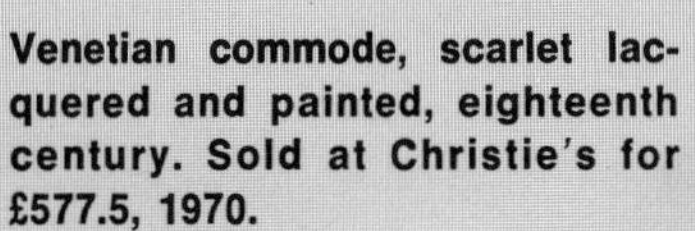

Venetian commode, scarlet lacquered and painted, eighteenth century. Sold at Christie's for £577.5, 1970.

THE ITALIAN BAROQUE

The seventeenth century in Italy produced a quantity of marble or *scagiola* topped tables which continue to be much admired. In May 1963 Christie's sold a mosaic marble top of a Florentine gilt-wood centre table, designed in the classical taste with Greek amphora, cameos and statues, for 600 guineas. The welter of ornament associated with the Italian Baroque is well illustrated by a 'river god' sidetable, the top inset with marble beneath which is the seated Ladon, which went through Sotheby's in May 1967. This profusely carved piece came from the Sala dei Fiurni in the Ducal Palace at Mantua and realised £3,900. Of course, not all furniture of this date commands such high prices; a pair of fine gilt-wood *torchères,* the stems carved with cherubs' masks and foliage scrolls, were sold for 800 guineas at Christie's in April 1970. Two years earlier, an elegant Tuscan walnut refectory table with single carved stretcher made 700 guineas. Nevertheless, the scarcity of good items is causing prices to rise, as is indicated by a fine sidetable carved with a *putto* and a 'river god' with *brèche violette* marble top, which fetched a mere 100 guineas at Christie's in March 1960.

Medals

Italian medals do not yet seem to appeal to the general collector, but rather to the dedicated numismatist who sees them as a close adjunct to his main interest. It is perhaps the only field left in which a broadly representative collection of seventeenth-century art can be formed without an enormous financial outlay. A good bronze portrait medal, or a religious scene by a known artist, will fetch up to £100, while those less perfect or less interesting are usually catalogued in groups of half a dozen or more and will average out at £5-£10 each.

Avoiding the Traps

The number of faked medals on the market makes the subject precarious for all who have not studied it first. But if this is done, the reward is twofold; the formation of a diverse and stimulating collecton for comparatively little, and the certainty, as ignorance is dispelled and further interest aroused, that prices will continue upwards. Sales of medals are standard and quite frequent events at the two major auction houses in England.

Arms and Armour

While sixteenth- and seventeenth-century Italian medals are relatively numerous, this is not true of contemporaneous arms and armour. Obviously much of what was produced has been destroyed and most of what has survived is in public, or well-known private, collections. A full armour of bright steel with unusual reinforcing plates and probably part of a garniture for field and tilt passed through Christie's in October 1969 and made 1,350 guineas. It dated from about 1560. In the same sale, a rare late-sixteenth-century stonebow with pearwood tiller and carved with a couchant lion above the trigger fetched 290 guineas. The piece illustrated is an interesting double-cock wheel lock mechanism struck with an armourer's mark; this was well sold at 450 guineas in July 1970. Two months prior to this, an early pair of flint-lock holster pistols with burr walnut stocks, steel furniture, and signed 'G. Frugone', realised 700 guineas. In brief, Italian arms and armour of good quality appear in the saleroom infrequently, and there is keen competition on each occasion.

TOM MILNES-GASKELL

A double-cock wheel lock mechanism, one of the few Italian arms to appear in London.